Hans J. Ullmann
Evamaria Ullmann
Dan Rice, D.V.M.

Spaniels

Everything About History, Purchase, Care, Nutrition, Training, and Behavior

Filled with Full-color Photographs

Illustrations by Michele Earle-Bridges

BARRON'S

2 CONTENTS

THE SPANIEL'S ORIGIN AND HISTORY

The word "spaniel" doesn't refer to a particular breed but rather to a dog type that includes several different breeds of medium-sized hunting dogs that share certain characteristics. The spaniels presented here are those dogs that are comfortable at their owners' sides in the sporting field, in field trials, conformation shows, obedience trials, and other competitive events. All are particularly valued as family companions. The breeds of toy spaniels are excluded.

Origin

Like other canines, spaniels originated from the wolf. In prehistoric times wolves were captured, domesticated, and kept by humans for many different purposes. From the time of cave dwellers to the present time, humans have shared their homes and hearths with dogs that have proven to be valuable partners. Spaniels and other hunting dogs have a purpose that evolved through careful selective breeding. That purpose is to assist their human counterparts gather meat for the family table.

Spaniel-type dogs appeared in early French writings and paintings and were referred to as *chiens d'Espagnol*, which means *dogs of Spain.*

An American Water Spaniel showing the typical heavy coat.

British writers of the same era used similar names such as *Spagnell, Spainell,* and *Spanyell.* Many canine historians ascribe the spaniel's origin to Spain, an assumption that may not be factual.

Welsh Springer Spaniels have their earliest known existence in Wales. English Springers have long been known in England and were developed from other British hunting breeds. Likewise, Field Spaniels, Cocker Spaniels, English Cocker Spaniels, and Sussex Spaniels were developed in various parts of the British Isles. The Irish Water Spaniel obviously originated in Ireland, and evidence points to France as the origin of the Clumber Spaniel that was later named for the Clumber region of England. The American Water Spaniel was developed in the United States.

Champion American Water Spaniel displaying beautiful balance and angulation.

Why, then, are these breeds called spaniels? Etymologically the word *spaniel* certainly refers to Spanish dogs. Some spaniel-type dogs were developed in Spain and perhaps some ancient Spanish hunting dogs were used in the gene pool of other European hunting dogs. That's just a general theory, but present-day spaniels were undoubtedly developed in many countries of Europe.

General Spaniel Description

Spaniels are medium-sized canines that are found in almost every conceivable color and pattern, and many possess great swimming prowess. They have excellent sensory abilities, are tough enough to withstand rough elements, and were developed to aid human hunters find, flush, and retrieve game birds. They are often divided into *land* and *water* spaniels, depending on their particular expertise.

Sporting dogs are multitalented and can usually be trained to perform many of the duties common to all hunting dogs. However, some were specifically developed to sniff out and point their quarry for human gunners, or in earlier times, for the falconer.

✔ The land retrievers were designed to retrieve wild turkeys, pheasants, quail, and other upland game birds and many of these dogs are also excellent pointers. Those upland sporting dogs include the land spaniels that are used to hunt woodcock. They were called "cocking spaniels," later shortened to Cocker Spaniels.

A parti-Cocker whose coat has been trimmed for comfort.

✔ English Springer Spaniels were named for their springing action when their quarry was located and the dogs were commanded to flush or *start* game birds for Greyhounds or falcons.

✔ Other sporting breeds were developed for retrieving ducks, geese, and other waterfowl, and they became water spaniels and water retrievers. Those breeds have webbed feet and have great swimming abilities. They differ from land spaniels in several features: Their coats are shorter, tighter, and more oily than the coats of land spaniels and naturally shed rather than absorb water. One shake of a water spaniel's body results in a nearly dry coat. The long coat of today's Cocker Spaniels can absorb several pounds of water and take hours to dry.

Size

European spaniels were divided into weight classes at the beginning of the nineteenth century, the smallest of which were the tiny companion pets that often were referred to as comforters, toys, or lap spaniels. They aren't primarily gun dogs although they roughly resemble some of their larger cousins in terms of coat and ear length.

Hunting spaniels that ranged between 14 and 28 pounds (6.3 and 12.7 kg) were called Cocker Spaniels, and those over 28 pounds (12.7 kg) were called Springer Spaniels, English Spaniels, or Field Spaniels. In those days if a spaniel outgrew its Cocker designation it might be called a Springer, Clumber, or Field Spaniel.

History and Countries of Origin

The origin of spaniels is subject to debate and probably never will be settled on any one continent or in a single country. Cocker Spaniels were separated from Springers in bench shows in 1833, and in 1892 the Cocker was given breed status in England. In the United States,

The English Springer Spaniel appeals to hunters and pet owners, and is a popular show dog.

American Cocker Spaniels were shown in the same classes with English Cockers until 1936 when the English Cocker Spaniel Club of America was formed. In 1946 the American Kennel Club (AKC) formally designated the English Cocker as a breed apart from the Cocker Spaniel (American Cocker). Today in the British Isles *Cocker Spaniel* refers to English Cockers. American Cocker Spaniels differ from English Cockers in type, size, and coloring.

Late in the nineteenth century a group of **English Springer Spaniels** was maintained as a purebred line in Shropshire and Norfolk, England. Toward the end of that century sportsmen conducted a series of field trials that included the different varieties of spaniels, all of which competed together. Afterward, the English

Springer Spaniels split from the other spaniels and in 1902 it was first recognized as a separate breed by The Kennel Club of England.

Clumber Spaniels were developed in the eighteenth century and are among the heaviest of the land spaniels. They were probably developed from old French land spaniels, and Basset Hounds are reported to have brought the heavy, long, and low profile to the Clumber. Clumber Spaniels were moved from France to England during the French Revolution and they were kept by the Duke of Newcastle at Clumber Park, where they got their name. Clumbers make remarkably good pets and have extremely sensitive noses but are too slow for most hunting enthusiasts.

Field Spaniels probably originated from crosses of Welsh Cocker with Sussex Spaniel.

Cocker Spaniel dam and puppy
waiting for playmate.

Until 1901 the Field Spaniel was considered more or less the same as the Cocker except that the Field Spaniel was a bit larger, weighing more than 25 pounds (11.3 kg).

American Water Spaniels were developed by sportsmen who weren't terribly concerned with pedigrees, so the time and place of origin aren't well documented. They were seen at the time of the Civil War and a few years later a fair number were found in the midwest of England, especially in lake and river country where waterfowl abound. The now extinct English Water Spaniel, the Irish Water Spaniel, and the Curly-Coated Retriever are probably the progenitors of that all-American breed that was and is a gundog with fantastic prowess in water retrieving.

Irish Water Spaniels are an ancient breed whose ancestors probably date to the Stone and Bronze Ages. Roman carvings of those eras depict dogs that closely resemble Irish Water Spaniels. In the late twelfth century dogs known as Shannon Spaniels, Irish Water Spaniels, Rat-Tail Spaniels, or Whip-Tail Spaniels were known in the River Shannon region of Ireland. Between 1834 and 1852 the Irish Water Spaniel officially gained recognition with a legendary dog of unknown pedigree named Boatswain.

Sussex Spaniels derive their name from Sussex, England and were developed in the late eighteenth and early nineteenth centuries. They have been used as trustworthy retrievers in England for years and are adept in rough country shooting. In spite of their quiet dispositions, they have never been popular in American homes and are considered among the rarest AKC breeds.

Welsh Springer Spaniels' history is sometimes traced to the earliest settlers of Brittany, Cornwall, Wales, Ireland, and Scotland, and may date to 7000 B.C. A dog closely resembling the Welsh Springer was known as the Agassian Hunting Dog in Great Britian and it is probably one of the forerunners of the land spaniels of that region. The breed's purity was sometimes questioned and the English and Welsh dogs were exhibited in the same classes in England, with the only difference being color. Welsh Springers are thought to have originally developed as red and white with no other colors being found. Animals of that type and color are depicted in tapestries woven during the Renaissance period and are found in various places in Europe and on the island of Malta.

PREPURCHASE CONSIDERATIONS

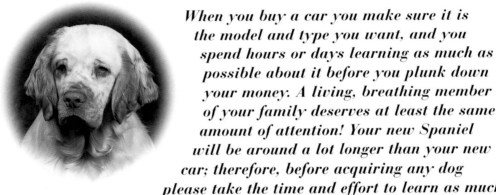

When you buy a car you make sure it is the model and type you want, and you spend hours or days learning as much as possible about it before you plunk down your money. A living, breathing member of your family deserves at least the same amount of attention! Your new Spaniel will be around a lot longer than your new car; therefore, before acquiring any dog please take the time and effort to learn as much as possible about the costs and pleasures of owning, feeding, training, exercising, and caring for the health of your new dog.

Is a Spaniel the Right Dog for You?

Don't underestimate the time and effort required to groom your spaniel. Would you be happier with a shorthaired breed that requires less time to groom? If a couple of hours of combing and brushing every week isn't your thing, a spaniel may be the wrong dog for you. And if you really want a great watchdog instead of a playful and affectionate companion, better consider a Doberman Pinscher or Rottweiler.

Be sure that the spaniel breed that you select is good fit for your lifestyle.

Delay your decision to purchase a spaniel until after you've reviewed your house and yard facilities. Will your dog be required to stay outside for extended periods of time? If so, a water- and windproof doghouse must be provided. Consider the cost of proper fencing if your backyard isn't already fenced dog-tight. Spaniels' heavy coats appear weatherproof but all dogs, regardless of their coat, must be protected from the elements. A doggy door into the kitchen might be another expense to think about.

What about vacations or weekend trips? Does your family take driving trips away from home? Can the spaniel accompany you? Always? Be honest about it. Will you ever need

Champion Cocker (Ruby) and Champion English Cocker (Stoney) at a field trial.

someone to care for him? Do you know your neighbors well enough to ask them to feed, exercise, and care for your companion? More important, are they qualified, trustworthy, and anxious to help out? If not please take time right now to find a reliable boarding kennel or professional pet-sitter. Visit the facility and observe the cleanliness and odors you find there. Talk to the staff; check the brand of food they serve. Consider providing your companion's regular food to prevent digestive upset that may be caused by dietary changes.

Choices Available

Sex

Many prospective owners have preconceived ideas about whether males or females make the best pets. One person will consider only a male and the next will accept only a female. In fact, very little difference is found between male and female pets if both are neutered (spayed or castrated). Neither is apt to be more affectionate, more trainable, more playful, less destructive, more responsive, or less aggressive. It's all personal choice and no one but you can decide which to buy.

Differences in sex arise mainly when intact animals are kept for pets. A bitch (female dog) in heat (estrus) will attract males for miles around. Uncastrated or intact males go crazy each time they perceive the scent of a female in season. Fighting among males, digging under fences, running loose, and car accidents are commonly the result of a bitch in season in the neighborhood.

Either castrated or intact males will sniff posts, hydrants, bushes, and trees as they walk, and they stall for time while their impatient owner stews. Most mature males raise a hind leg and squirt a few drops of urine on every spot that was ever used by another dog. Unfortunately, that *territorial marking* habit is deeply ingrained in canine heritage and can't be eliminated, no matter how hard you try. Castrated males and females that have been spayed also mark their territory with urine. It is simply a method of leaving a scent that is peculiar to that individual.

Naturally, a female spaniel is chosen if the owner is planning to raise puppies but that is unlikely and inadvisable for the majority of pet

A brace of English Springer Spaniels.

buyers. Buying and keeping an intact male to be used for stud purposes is also a bad idea.

Naming Your Spaniel

Ideally, a name should contain two distinctly different-sounding syllables that when pronounced together have a sound all their own. The name should be as short as possible, and should never sound like anyone else's name or a command that you are planning to use. For instance, if you own a male named *Dandy*, don't name your new female *Candy*. *Joe* is a nice short name but it sounds like the command *No!* Practice saying the chosen name outside when your spaniel is not around. Our choices for the dogs used in this book are *Bingo* for the male and *Cindy* for the female.

The New Home and Family

Analyze your living quarters, your family's interest, and especially your habits. Before you decide on a new companion, consider when and how much time you will devote to caring for your new pal. Although a spaniel is an adaptable pet, the new addition must have exercise and training. You can't feed him and push him out the door to fend for himself. He has tremendous energy and ambition; he is an

CHECKLIST

Ownership

1 Are you financially able to afford Bingo's annual maintenance needs? These include veterinary bills for preventive health measures such as vaccinations, examinations, and worm checks. A good, premium dog food will be required as well as insurance, license fees, and housing costs. Can you afford necessary training classes or professional trainer fees if needed?

2 Will you always have patience with Bingo? Will you teach him good manners and respect for humans and their property? Are you certain that you have the necessary knowledge about dogs to earn Bingo's respect and sufficient competence to train him adequately? If the answer is no, are you willing, and do you have the time, to master that competence?

3 Will you modulate your voice, never lose your temper, never yell or physically reprimand your pet?

4 Do you demand proficiency or perfection in yourself and your human associates? If so, you are likely to be dictatorial in your actions and commands to pets and will likely be a terrible spaniel owner.

5 Socialization is necessary for Bingo. This means becoming accustomed to other dogs as well as people. Do you have the time and interest to introduce him daily to strangers?

6 When Bingo makes a mistake, how will you react? If he chews up a valuable rug or your favorite pair of shoes, who will you blame?

7 How many hours will Bingo be left alone every day?

8 Do you like to walk, jog, or run for exercise? Can you take Bingo with you? Or are you a couch potato who would rather sit before the TV?

9 Will you learn all you can about Bingo's nutritional and exercise needs and assure that he'll receive a good measure of both?

If you can't see yourself taking responsibility for your new spaniel please don't start out on this venture. Be sure your priorities are sound and your thoughts are clear. Bingo will be a wonderful companion only if he has an owner who is responsible, patient, and understanding.

exuberant, vital, and playful puppy. If you have a large, properly fenced yard, that's fine but it only assures the space to exercise. Spaniels need human company; play is a participation sport that requires you to initiate his exercise.

All dogs' heritage is that of living together in families or *packs*. In order to produce the kind of spaniel you really want you must take the commanding role as leader of the pack. You must train Bingo to focus his attention on you and you must respond comfortably and quickly. Every time he looks at you, answer by giving him some instruction. Perhaps it will be only a hand motion to come to you for some petting, or maybe it will be pointing to a tennis ball for him to bring to you. Or maybe you will pick up his Frisbee and toss it a few times or put on his leash and take him for a short outing.

If you haven't a couple of hours a day to dedicate to Bingo's needs, perhaps you should consider a bowl of guppies for pets.

Puppy or Adult?

The answer to this question requires a lot of thought, and planning as well. A puppy is great fun to watch and interact with. Nothing brings greater joy than the antics of a clumsy spaniel puppy scampering about and chewing on your toes. Remember that Bingo's puppy awkwardness is quickly transformed into a polished, knowledgeable, well-trained hunting dog or companion pet that focuses on you and responds to you almost without hesitation.

Downside

The downside of puppy owning is the amount of time and effort you spend house-training, leash-training, fundamental obedience training, and socializing. Another feature of owning a puppy is the actual out-of-pocket cost. Vaccinations are usually continued for a lifetime but initial costs are considerably more. Puppy food is more expensive than a maintenance diet. Puppies need to be checked for worms more frequently than older dogs and they get into trouble fairly often. Medical bills always seem higher when a puppy is in the house.

Rescued Dogs

An alternative approach might be attractive. Connect on the Internet with the national or local rescue groups for your particular breed of spaniel. You will receive assistance from those groups. A wait of a few weeks may be required

An Irish Water Spaniel holding a favorite toy in his mouth.

to get a rescued dog but it will arrive with a clean bill of health, vaccinated, neutered, de-wormed, and in most cases, checked for heartworms.

A rescued dog isn't the answer to everyone's needs, but if you can forgo the joys of owning a puppy, a rescued dog may be a viable alternative. An older dog will bond securely with its new owner although the process may take a little longer. It may already be trained to walk on a leash, come when its name is called, maybe even heel for you, and if it has had a good owner in the past, it might even sit and stay.

A brief respite for these Field Spaniels, who are full of energy most of the day.

Adopting

Shelters often have spaniels of various sorts for adoption as well. The possibility of acquiring a problem dog from a shelter is greater than if you adopt one from a rescue group. This is because the people who cause problems in dogs often can't deal with those problems and take the fastest and surest way out: They either dump the dog in a strange neighborhood and it is picked up by the pound or they surrender their problem dog directly to a pound. In either case, the shelter will keep the dog for a few days, then offer it for adoption. Usually, sufficient time hasn't passed for anyone to recognize or analyze the problems of such a dog.

Adult Dogs

If your dream is to own a good spaniel companion you might try an adult spaniel first, but be sure you have the right to return the dog within a reasonable time with no penalty applicable, because you may change your mind in the first couple of weeks. A spaniel of any age will appreciate its new home if you make it comfortable and don't demand too much too soon. Be patient but be positive. Don't give up without a struggle but don't accept an adult dog in spite of all his bad habits with the idea that you can work them all out.

New Puppy

If your choice is a new puppy, several other considerations apply. He should be at least 10 weeks old and should be sufficiently independent and mature to withstand the change of environment. He should be properly vaccinated, be eating well, and have a clean bill of health.

Spend at least a couple of brief visits with the breeder before making your selection. Ask him or her all the questions that come to mind about spaniel puppies in general and your selection in particular because a puppy's personality is already partially established during his first few months of life. Satisfy yourself that the puppy's dam and siblings are disease-free and ask permission to take your puppy to your veterinarian for a pre-purchase exam. Ask the veterinarian about personality testing and obtain a recommendation for diet and future preventive health care.

Choosing Your Spaniel Puppy

✔ Choose your particular spaniel breed, read the conformation standards, and learn its most important features and most common faults.

✔ Go on the Internet to the national breed club's web site, contact the secretary, and get the name of several reputable breeders in your area.

✔ Attend a dog show, meet and talk to breeders; ask them if they have puppies for sale.

✔ Call the breeders and find at least three litters that will be ready for adoption within the next couple of weeks and make an appointment to visit one the next day.

✔ Compare as many puppies as possible; consider their physical features, conformation, and personality.

✔ Either sex will work for you if all else is equal. Take your time and make this important decision thoughtfully and without prejudice.

✔ This is to be your companion, your responsibility, so make the first trip to each breeder's by yourself.

✔ Equip yourself with an aluminum soda can into which you've put a couple marbles and sealed with tape.

A lonely American Water Spaniel puppy seeking a friendly face to lick.

=== TIP ===

When Should You Purchase Your Dog?

✔ After you've consulted your family and everyone is in agreement.

✔ After you've arranged schedules so someone is home most of the time, at least for several weeks.

✔ During a season of stable weather when a minimum of commotion and confusion prevails.

✔ After you've read all about the spaniel of your choice and how to take care of it.

✔ After you've prepared your yard and provided the necessary shelter and fence.

✔ After you've surveyed your home and removed all obstacles and dangers from a spaniel's reach.

✔ After you've asked a neighbor or responsible dog-sitter, or located a boarding kennel to take care of Bingo when you travel.

Welsh Springer Spaniel dams and their puppies happily await their owner.

✔ When you enter the breeder's home don't immediately go to the kennel room. First look at the dam's pedigree and AKC registration, certificates of eye examinations, Orthopedic Foundation for Animals (OFA) certification of her hips, and any other health-related documents available. Then, after being introduced to the dam, handle her, pet her, and look into her eyes. If she is shy, won't stand petting, or is otherwise timid, don't bother looking at her puppies.

✔ Ask the breeder if he has one of the dam's previous litter's puppies that you might also see. If it is a nice, agreeable spaniel, ask to see the new puppies, but don't immediately step into their midst.

✔ Watch the puppies from across the room, through the crack of a door if possible. Their playful antics are humorous but that's not why you're spying on them from afar.

✔ Watch for a puppy that is curious, playful, ambitious, but one that's not a bully.

✔ Make a mental note of any that are notably timid, hiding behind the nesting box, and slow to respond to their siblings.

✔ Walk up to the puppies and note those that run away and hide and those that turn, watch you for a few seconds, then begin going after your shoelaces.

✔ Make a mental note of the puppies that weren't a bit afraid when you walked into the room.

✔ Sit down on the floor and note which puppies climb on your lap and try to lick your face. Don't pick up any, and for the time being, don't even pet one.

Documents to Obtain with the Puppy

1. Bill of sale and receipt for your payment.
2. Vaccination certificates including revaccination date suggestions.
3. Worm check certification with date of recommended recheck.
4. Pedigree.
5. AKC registration application (puppy registration papers).
6. Replacement or money-back guarantee in case the puppy has a health problem.
7. Diet including brand, amount, and frequency of feeding.
8. Possible guarantee related to hereditary diseases such as hip dysplasia, PRA, and others.
9. Any contract you made relative to spaying, neutering, showing, or breeding your dog.

A happy Champion Sussex Spaniel showing off for his audience.

✔ After they have become accustomed to your presence, with the breeder's permission, roll your marble-filled soda can across the floor. Some will be frightened and run for cover. Some will be startled but stand their ground. Then they will cock their heads until the can stops, then walk or run to it to investigate. Make a mental note of those puppies that showed no fear but were first startled, then followed the can.

✔ Ask the breeder to fault the conformation of the one or two puppies that you've noted and if he tells you the puppy or puppies are pretty good examples of the breed, ask him to record the puppies as your first choice(s) of his litter.

After visiting at least a couple of other litters, ask your spouse or a friend to accompany you to help make the final selection. When you make your choice you will be asked to leave a deposit if the puppy isn't quite ready to leave its siblings. Agree on the date to pick up your new companion and you're almost ready to complete your ownership of a new spaniel puppy.

Ask the puppy's breeder what vaccinations the puppy has received and ask to have a copy of the certification of vaccinations, the name of the veterinarian who gave them, and the date the next vaccination is due. Also be sure you get information relative to the puppy's latest worm test, what he is being fed, how much, and the specific feeding schedule.

DESCRIPTION OF NINE SPANIEL BREEDS

If you are curious about or if you are seriously considering showing or breeding your spaniel you should read and digest the entire breed standard before you purchase your puppy. The AKC publishes a new edition of **The Complete Dog Book** *every few years and it is an excellent reference for all recognized breeds. However, standards do change periodically and information that was current a few years ago may no longer apply. For the latest breed standard go online to the AKC and follow the prompts to find the complete and current breed standard for your spaniel.*

American Water Spaniel

This medium-sized American breed sports a tightly curled or marcel (uniform waves), solid brown, waterproof coat with sufficiently dense undercoat to insulate against cold weather and water. It stands 15 to 18 inches (38 to 45.7 cm) tall and weighs 25 to 40 pounds (11 to 18 kg). Its eye color ranges from yelllowish brown to brown or hazel. Lemon-colored, yellow eyes are a disqualifying feature. Its nose rubber is dark brown or black and its bite is scissor or level.

A Cocker Spaniel that has been groomed to perfection for a dog show.

Its feet are tightly webbed and well padded. This spaniel is at home retrieving upland game birds such as ducks and geese.

The American Water Spaniel was recognized by the AKC in 1940 and it is first and last an athletic, solidly built, well-muscled gundog that is full of strength and quality. It doesn't point but marks game with great precision and may make multiple retrieves without shooters' direction.

The American Water Spaniel usually is gentle and friendly with children but reserved with strangers and an excellent watchdog. It is intelligent, reasonably easily trained, and, like

An American Water Spaniel practicing retrieving with a bird wing.

most sporting breeds, it requires significant exercise and wants human and canine socialization from puppyhood. Typically, the American Water Spaniel is a sensitive, one-person

The Clumber Spaniel was once referred to as the "retired gentleman's hunting dog."

dog that isn't as eager to please as many other spaniels. It does not thrive on harsh treatment, which may lead to fear-biting or timidity and separation anxiety. Some have been reported to be territorially aggressive and some require extensive training to overcome chewing, digging, and jumping tendencies.

Clumber Spaniel

Clumbers' coats are white with lemon or orange markings, dense, straight, and flat with ample undercoat to resist foul weather. This spaniel stands 17 to 20 inches (43 to 50.8 cm) tall and weighs a hefty 55 to 85 pounds (25 to 39 kg); it is slightly longer than its height. Its eyes are dark amber and its nose rubber varies from brown to rose or cherry in color. A scissors bite is preferred.

The general build of the Clumber is long, low, and heavy. It is a powerful spaniel with a massive and powerful body. This may slow it down a bit but it makes it more useful in heavy cover and it's an enthusiastic hunter. It's temperament is sometimes reserved with strangers but it is a loyal and affectionate companion and is never hostile or shy.

The Clumber Spaniel was registered with the AKC in 1878, which is six years before the actual founding of the AKC. That seeming impossibility is explained by the stud books that were accepted as the basis for establishment of the *Stud Book Register*, published in 1887 and continuously since that time.

The ancient lineage of the Clumber may be the reason for the dog's solemn, aristocratic attitude. It is intelligent, easily trained and controlled, and a natural retriever. It possesses extraordinary endurance in the field and has a

This Cocker's favorite Christmas present—a pheasant dummy.

superior scenting ability. It is an excellent water retriever and a workhorse among spaniels. In the bargain, a Clumber makes a fine house pet with modest requirements for regular exercise consisting of long walks and interactive games. It is quite proficient in obedience and tracking competitions and many consent to live in apartments, even though they might prefer country life with its hunting challenges. Insufficient exercise may result in obesity that will reduce the Clumber's life expectancy.

Cocker Spaniel

Cocker Spaniels are found in several color varieties: black, ASCOB (any solid color other than black), ASCOB and tan, and parti-color (two or more definite, well-defined colors, one of which is white). Roan Cockers are shown as parti-colors. The colors and varieties, each with its particular markings, are complex but are amply covered in the breed standard. Their coats are silky, flat, or slightly wavy with sufficient undercoat for protection. Ideal height is 14 inches for bitches and 15 inches for males (35.5 and 38 cm); they weigh 24 to 28 pounds (10.9 to 12.7 kg). Cockers have brown eyes, liver to black nose rubber with darker colors preferred. Scissors bite is required.

The Cocker (American Cocker) is the smallest of the AKC sporting breeds and is chosen by many small-dog enthusiasts for a superior family companion. Typically, the well-bred Cocker has a cheerfully sweet disposition and is easily trained with patience and gentle perseverance. It must receive plenty of human socialization to develop to its full potential as a companion. It is playful, trustworthy, and adaptable but is commonly quite sensitive and does not do well with harsh treatment. Its family role includes both adult and children companionship and it will probably thrive among groups of playing children. It adjusts quickly to training and may excel in obedience, flyball, agility, and simple tricks. In years past, this fine but vulnerable dog has been overbred by puppy mills, which have produced noisy, nervous, untrustworthy puppies that are nearly the exact opposite of the typical well-bred Cockers.

The American Cocker Spaniel retained its position in the Sporting Group when it was split from the English Toy Spaniel, and gained recognition as a separate breed when it was recognized by the AKC in 1935 as a different breed from the English Cocker Spaniel.

An English Cocker waiting her turn at field trial.

Differences between the English Cocker Spaniel's conformation and that of the American Cocker are rather dramatic. The English muzzle is longer, the head is slightly flatter, and the eyes are less prominent. The English Cocker's body is taller, heavier, and more solid. The English Cocker does not have the profusion of belly coat and leg furnishing found on the American Cocker.

The English Cocker is an active, high-energy sporting dog that covers ground and penetrates dense cover with ease. As a pet its temperament is merry, affectionate, and loyal. It thrives on hunting and country living but makes an excellent companion dog and usually does well in obedience, tracking, agility, and flyball competition. The English Cocker is a happy, fun-loving pet that needs significant exercise to burn excess energy that may not be furnished by sedentary families. Its manners around children are exemplary and human socialization is quite important for this dog to develop into the very best companion possible.

The English Cocker Spaniel Club of America was formed in 1935 to promote the English Cocker, which had been split from Springers in 1892. AKC recognition for the English Cocker came in 1947.

English Cocker Spaniel

English Cockers are exhibited in many colors that include parti-colors, roans, and ticked, black, liver, or shades of red. Solid colors include black, liver, or shades of red with and without tan markings. Refer to the breed standard for a full explanation of colors. Their coats are silky and flat or wavy. Their height is 16 to 17 inches for males (40.6 to 43.1 cm) and 15 to 16 inches for females (38.1 to 40.6 cm); their weight is 28 to 34 pounds for males (12.7 to 15.4 kg) and 26 to 32 pounds (11.8 to 14.5 kg) for females. Their eyes are dark brown and hazel in liver and parti-colors. Black is the preferred color of the nose rubber but brown is permissible in livers and parti-colors. A scissors bite is preferred over a level bite; undershot or overshot bites are penalized.

Field Spaniel

Field Spaniels are shown in black, liver, golden liver, roan, or any of those colors with tan points. Their coats are dense, water-repellent, moderately long, silky, flat, or slightly

A beautiful Field Spaniel shows off a fine, immaculately groomed coat.

wavy. The ideal size for males is 18 inches (45.7 cm) and 17 inches for bitches (43.1 cm), and they are slightly longer than tall. Weights range from 35 to 50 pounds (15.9 to 22.7 kg); their eye color is dark hazel to dark brown. The nose rubber is light to dark brown or black. Either a scissor or level bite is permissible, but scissor is preferred.

The Field Spaniel is a hunter with good balance of body, solid bone, and firm musculature. It's moderate speed, great agility, and endurance combined with good balance makes this spaniel a good choice for either a companion or gundog. It is an active, friendly companion that is usually eager to please its owner. It is typically reserved around strangers but makes an excellent companion for children of the family. It may bark at an interloper but isn't likely to attack. Its love of water may create rather untidy drinking habits and its

retrieving heritage will cause it to carry objects about and leave them all over the house. A Field Spaniel is an intelligent and active dog that requires a significant amount of exercise and diverse training to prevent boredom and mischievousness. It is quite trainable, and continual human socialization and light obedience or Canine Good Citizen training will help to produce a good, well-rounded companion.

Field Spaniels' history and development was totally intertwined with the Welsh Cocker, Sussex Spaniel, and of course the Springer and Cocker. Together with the Cocker, it was introduced to America in the early 1880s and was finally recognized as a distinct breed. It suffered near extinction in the early 1900s and wasn't seen in the American dog fancy until it was reintroduced to the United States in the mid-1960s. Field Spaniels have gained modest popularity in the past decade.

One fancy English Springer all stacked up.

English Springer Spaniel

English Springer Spaniels are black or liver with white markings or mostly white with liver or black markings, tricolor (black and white or liver and white with tan markings), blue, or liver roan. Off colors such as lemon, red, or orange are heavily penalized. Their body coat is fine and glossy, flat or wavy, and sufficiently dense to be waterproof. Their height is 20 inches for males and 19 inches for females (50.8 and 48.6 cm); their weight ranges from 49 to 55 pounds (22.3 to 25 kg). The preferred eye color is dark hazel in liver-colored dogs and black or dark brown in black and white spaniels. Their nose rubbers are either black or liver colored, depending on the coat color. The bite of the English Springer must be scissor, and any deviation from that standard is severely penalized.

The English Springer is a medium-sized sporting breed that is of necessity well balanced in bone and musculature, its length being the same as its height. It is well proportioned and energetic, has speed, endurance, and enthusiasm in the field. Any lacking these hunting qualities are penalized.

A field-bred Springer isn't apt to do well in a conformation ring. By the same measure, a conformation-bred Springer may not perform well in the hunting field. Either type can be an exceptional companion pet, a cheerful, happy dog with a terrific sense of humor. It is a great children's companion, affectionate and playful, and with a bit of training may excel in Agility or Flyball games. It is not a reliable watchdog but may bark an alarm when a stranger approaches. Although it is generally considered a high-energy companion, it can do well with more modest exercise. Generally, a Springer will thrive on backyard exercise, daily walks, ball games, Frisbee, and scenting games. With sufficient human socialization, this dog is quite adaptable to a variety of environments and will excel as a companion.

During the nineteenth century Springers and Cockers were often born in the same litter, but in 1902 the Kennel Club of England recognized the English Springer as a separate breed. The American Spaniel Club was founded in 1880 and in 1924 the English Springer Spaniel Field Trial Association became the original American parent club of the breed. In 1927 the AKC breed standard was adopted and the English Springer has continued to be a popular field and companion dog.

Irish Water Spaniel

Irish Water Spaniels' uniformly solid liver-colored coats are double to insulate against the weather and cold water. The dense, tightly

Irish Water Spaniels display their tight, curly, waterproof coats.

curled ringlets cover nearly the entire dog with longer hair on the lower chest. This waterproof coat requires no trimming for show or gun work. The tail of the Irish Water Spaniel is called ratlike; it tapers to a fine point with short curls at the root and ending in a smooth hair covering as if it has been clipped. This breed's characteristic topknot of long loose curls grows into a peak between the eyes and falls over the ear tops. Irish Water Spaniel males stand 22 to 24 inches (55.8 to 61 cm) and bitches 21 to 23 inches (52.5 to 57.5 cm). Their eyes are hazel; dark hazel is preferred.

Their nose rubbers are liver colored and their bites are either scissor or level.

Although this Irish dog is often called the clown of the spaniels, the title is unearned. This dog often has clownish tendencies but this tallest of the spaniels is all business in the field. It is loyal to its handlers and friends and often feared by strangers. This spaniel is a swimming machine, deep chested, powerful, and muscular; it is a true athlete with all the characteristics of that title. It isn't timid but is often reserved with strangers. Shyness or aggression is penalized because a hunting dog's temperament must be stable.

This Sussex Spaniel is bored with a life that lacks action.

The disposition of the Irish Water Spaniel is characterized by inquisitiveness, alertness, and a genuine zest for life. It is happiest when in the water but it has a desire to please and is usually very cooperative and trainable. This dog is known as a one-person dog and it may refuse commands given by others in the family. It is best situated in a family with older, knowledgeable children, and is a strong, self-confident companion. It is said to be stubborn and have a mind of its own but is usually not human-aggressive, although it may become aggressive toward other dogs under some circumstances. The importance of both canine socialization and human socialization cannot be overstated. If signs of problems arise, professional training may be required to curtail snapping or timidity and suspiciousness.

The first Westminster Kennel Club Show in 1877 had four Irish Water Spaniels entered, but time hasn't increased this breed's presence in the United States and it is now ranked among the rarest of breeds chosen for companions and hunting dogs.

Sussex Spaniel

Sussex Spaniels' coats are of a uniform golden liver color and abundant, flat, or slightly wavy with no tendency to curl. Sussex Spaniels stand 13 to 15 inches (33 to 38 cm) and weigh 35 to 45 pounds (16 to 20.5 kg). Their eyes are hazel in color, their nose rubbers are liver colored, and their bite must be scissors; any other bite is a fault.

Massive-appearing Sussex Spaniels are slightly longer than tall. They were once satisfactory sporting companions for English hunting on foot in rough country; however, they lack sufficient speed for most sportsmen and have become a rarity in the United States in spite of their excellent scenting ability. They possess good musculature and their powerful and strong-boned legs tend to be slightly bowed in front. Their rolling gait is deliberate but not clumsy.

The Sussex Spaniel has a somber expression but that countenance hides a dry sense of humor. Its appearance leads a novice to believe that it is lazy but its action out-of-doors is nothing short of amazing. It is a high-energy companion that requires vigorous exercise to thrive. Lacking sufficient attention to exercise, the Sussex will become bored and express that boredom in all the usual ways, such as destructiveness, barking, separation anxiety, and general nuisance activity. If you can't spare plenty of time for the Sussex, it isn't the dog for you. It is generally an easygoing companion but it is stubborn and assertive at times. Steady, consistent, fair training methods will overcome the stubborn traits. It is often dominant around other dogs and needs extensive attention to human and canine socialization.

The Sussex Spaniel was kept for hunting in England in the eighteenth century and the breed was among the first ten recognized by the AKC. It was admitted to the club's studbook in 1884 but has never gained significant popularity as either a pet or hunting companion. The Sussex Spaniel's somber appearance belies its merry disposition that can't be faulted.

Welsh Springer Spaniel

Welsh Springer Spaniels' coats are waterproof, dense, straight, and flat, never wiry or wavy. Their color is a pattern of any kind as long as it is rich red and white—no other colors are acceptable. Males stand 18 to 19 inches (45.7 to 48.3 cm) and bitches 17 to 18 inches (43.1 to 45.7 cm); weights range from 35 to 45 pounds (15.9 to 20.5 kg). Eye color is medium to dark brown, and yellow eyes are heavily penalized. Nose rubber is black or brown and pink nose rubber is severely penalized. A scissor bite is preferred and an undershot jaw is severely penalized.

A Welsh Springer stands focused, anxiously awaiting the next retrieve.

The Welsh Springer is a high-energy sporting dog that requires daily and vigorous exercise to thrive in any environment, regardless of whether it is in a hunting or companion dog home. It is extremely active and makes a fine pet for children and young adults alike, but lack of exercise will lead to obesity and laziness. The Welsh Springer is a happy and willing pet with a loyal and affectionate outlook on life. It is somewhat reserved around strangers but is rarely timid or unfriendly. Human socialization, consistent training methods, and leadership training are extremely important for this dog and should be continued throughout life.

The popularity in its native land wavered during the 1800s but gained popularity in the latter part of the century in the United States.

AKC recognition was awarded the breed in 1906 but during the years of World War I and World War II, the breed faded and it's probable that none were alive in America by the end of World War II. This changed in 1949 when importation from Great Britain revived the breed and the Welsh Springer Spaniel club of America was formed in 1961.

This well-balanced, active dog is as long as its height and is known for its endurance and hard muscle. Its strong, well boned body is not coarse but is powerful and able to cover a great deal of ground in a hurry with a minimum of energy expenditure. Its temperament is affectionate and loyal but reserved with strangers. It is never unfriendly, shy, or timid, and it is a devoted family companion and hunting partner.

SUPPLIES FOR YOUR SPANIEL

Acquiring a family spaniel is a major step that requires some major thought and planning. The actual purchase of Cindy might be the least costly of your total expenditures. Expenses go on even after you've arranged for her housing and dog-proof backyard fence and a doggy door leading into the kitchen. Next come the many products sold by pet supply stores. Buy the most necessary items first.

Necessary Equipment

Don't start out with an empty shopping buggy and a full wallet and end up with the opposite. Cindy doesn't need everything you see. If possible, take an experienced dog owner with you, preferably one who has raised a similar puppy to adulthood.

Collar and tag: The first items on the Checklist are easily selected. Cindy will require a nylon or leather buckle collar that will be worn all the time you aren't training her. Hang her identification tag on it and after training it can be used for walks as well. Also buy a chain training collar that fits her with a little growing room. Ask your friend who is shopping with you (or a knowledgeable clerk) to show you how to put it on Cindy's neck so it does not

A liver and white English Cocker Spaniel.

CHECKLIST

Necessary Supplies
- ✔ Collars
- ✔ Identification tag
- ✔ Head halter
- ✔ Leashes
- ✔ Crate
- ✔ Food and water bowls
- ✔ Metal combs
- ✔ Stiff brush
- ✔ Mat splitter
- ✔ Stair gate
- ✔ Portable pen
- ✔ Canine shampoo
- ✔ Canine toothpaste and brush
- ✔ Dog food

Regardless of her sad appearance, this Sussex isn't really unhappy.

Proper placement of a nylon training collar.

choke her when it tightens (see Collar and Leash Training, page 64).

Head halter: You can forgo the purchase of a head halter until you've seen if she adapts well to the training collar and if she behaves fairly well during her training. If she is a bit obstinate or if she is a real handful and continually pulls at the leash, buy the head halter. It is the most humane training tool you will ever use.

Training leash: You will need a training leash to match the buckle collar. It should be 4 or 6 feet long (1.2 or 1.8 m) and should be of medium to heavy nylon material. If you want to buy an expanding walking leash at the same time, choose a medium strength, spring-loaded leash that will lengthen or shorten quickly when a button is pushed on the handle. This leash will be an excellent investment for your dog's socialization with strangers and other dogs.

Dog crate: Dog crates are usually fashioned from fiberglass and are available in many sizes.

This Champion Welsh Springer playfully awaits the next ball game.

Pick one that will accommodate Cindy as an adult and allow her to stand up and turn around comfortably. The crate should be equipped with a foolproof latch; it should be properly ventilated with a carrying handle on top. This will be her cave, her den or refuge, and her favorite sleeping place. The crate is well accepted and not unkind if its use is not abused.

Bowls: Food and water bowls of stainless steel are best. Two sets are suggested so that one set can be cleaned in the dishwasher. Again, the specific size should be sufficient to hold an adult spaniel's meals. Look for special spaniel bowls that have a top that is smaller than the bottom to keep long ears clean. Soft plastic bowls should not be used because the chemicals from which they are made can leach into the food contents. Take care not to buy ceramic or clay bowls that may contain lead. Glass bowls can be broken and should be avoided.

Combs and brushes: Choose a metal comb with teeth that are sufficiently wide to allow regular combing without pulling. A second *flea comb* can be purchased now as well. It is a similar comb but the teeth are quite close together. It is used to help find fleas if you suspect these pesky parasites.

Buy a good-quality grooming brush. Check the sharpness of the bristles to be sure they won't scratch or abrade Cindy's tender skin.

A Cocker puppy waiting for supper.

If you try it on your own head, you should be able to make the proper selection.

Mat splitter: A mat splitter is a must for grooming your spaniel. Use it anytime a mat has formed in her coat, especially in her ear hair, between her toes, and in the long feathering of her belly. Your shopping companion or a knowledgeable clerk will show you how to use it properly.

Gate: A stair gate is a must if Cindy is a puppy and your home has stairs. The dog gate should be constructed in such a way that she can't trap her head in it or injure herself in other ways. A stair gate is very important for homes with exposed basement stairs because clumsy puppies can easily fall.

X-pen: A portable pen (X-pen) is a handy way to limit her movement in your home where her presence is not wanted until she is house-trained and trustworthy enough to have the run of the house. It can also be used at night instead of a crate as a sleeping place if furnished with a warm blanket or dog bed.

Shampoo: Canine shampoo is superior to any human product because it has been acid-base balanced to match the normal pH of her skin. It is probably most important if Cindy is to spend significant time outside and bathing is performed on a regular basis.

Toothpaste: Canine toothpaste has special flavoring that's pleasing to Cindy's palate and that will assure success. Either a special dog toothbrush or little latex brushes that fit over your finger can be used; both can be found in the pet supply shop.

Food

Dog food will be discussed later. It appears here only because a pet supply shop is an excellent place to buy it (see Spaniel Nutrition, page 53).

Bedding

No bed is needed if Cindy is taught to sleep in her crate. A folded blanket or large towel makes an excellent bed for her. It can be taken from the crate and washed whenever necessary. During teething, some puppies chew up everything in sight, so use expendable bedding. Cardboard boxes and wicker baskets are sometimes used but are rarely advisable because of a puppy's propensity to chew and the difficulty of cleaning the bed in case it is soiled.

Put Cindy's crate in your bedroom for the first few nights so she can hear and see you. Open the crate and allow it to sit open for

This quartet of Cocker puppies are cooking up some mischief.

several hours with an attractive chew toy inside. Pick up Cindy and place her gently inside the crate with a particularly yummy treat, then close the gate and walk away without lingering. Return a few minutes later and open the gate without fanfare. Do this for increasing time periods until she is content to be left alone in her crate for an hour or two. It can be moved to any room if she needs to be confined at other times. She will seek her crate for a nap within a few days and soon will be found there anytime she isn't under your feet or when she wants to escape noisy children for an hour.

A crate will allow her sleeping place to be readily moved to other homes, the car's back-seat, and motel rooms, and she will immediately recognize it as her proper sleeping place—however, it should never be used as punishment. It must be recognized as a good place to go to, a warm comfortable place to nap or gnaw on a rawhide chewy.

The Sussex facial expression belies its action in the field.

UNDERSTANDING SPANIELS

Behavioral patterns of spaniels are a result of several combined influences, one of which is copying their progenitors' (wolves) instinctive habits. These hereditary habits include circling before lying down, burying bones for future reference, urine-marking posts and stones along pathways, defecating a distance from their dens, and of course the all-important pack thinking.

Canine Adaptability

Wolflike genetic influences still persist and are especially seen in feral dog colonies that live in various parts of the world. However, those hereditary instincts have been diluted during the thousands of generations that humans have selectively bred domestic dogs. Our canine friends are proficient in performing certain duties in certain ways that relate to easing the workload of their human leaders. Dogs are perhaps the most malleable creatures on earth. All have descended from similar species of wolves but today's dogs range in size from the diminutive Chihuahua to the massive Mastiff or the gigantic Irish Wolfhound. They range in types

A Champion Welsh Springer with her soft brown eyes and black nose.

from working dogs that earn their livelihood by herding and protecting great flocks of livestock to tiny pooches that are loved only for their companionable natures. Spaniels, of course, were originated to help their owners collect meat for the human table and for their participation in the sport that grew from that discipline.

The spaniel type evolved through careful observation and selection of dogs with particular talents and physical qualities that made them ideal for seeking, finding, flushing, and retrieving game birds. Hereditarily, spaniels are still pack animals but the difference between a pack of wolves and a family of humans is that Cindy has taken a position that's far removed from the leader of a pack. She looks to her human leader to provide shelter, food, instruction, training, grooming, play, and affection.

This English Springer shows a style of grooming that is cared for easily.

Cindy lives at the feet of all her human companions but she does so willingly.

Body Language and What It Means

Dogs have always altered their body postures to express themselves to other canines but domestication taught them to include the human in this circle of companions. A friendly Cocker will willingly tell you by her facial expression and wagging tail that she wants petting. Or under different circumstances, she may express anger by pulling her lips back and showing her teeth and, when combined with a low growl, you know that she means business. Body language signals the observant hunter

when Cindy is on a hot or cold trail. When she picks up a quail scent on the wind, her muzzle drops lower and she moves toward the most concentrated odor of quail, moving toward it ever slower and more deliberately. Her tail action signals that she's serious and a gun had better be unlimbered.

Ears: The ears of a spaniel are too pendulous to be pointed but Cindy's are raised slightly when she is concentrating on something of interest. By the facial expression and ear position, an observant owner can detect what action or mischief the pet is contemplating at any given moment.

Tongue: The tongue of a spaniel is used much as its wolf ancestor's to display affection for its siblings or mother, except that Cindy includes her human family as well. Nothing I am aware of even comes close to the friendly face-licking a child or dedicated adult receives from his wonderful spaniel pal. That special greeting is bestowed whenever Cindy is allowed to meet her friends on her level. If an adult doesn't bend down to receive the greeting, Cindy will probably jump up as high as she can to encourage bending. A comic strip child recently said, "My dog loves me so much that she greets me with loving doggy kisses, even if I've left her home alone all day."

Circling: Circling a spot on the carpet before lying down is seen in many of our spaniel companions. That habit probably grew out of the wolf's need to first trample the grass and flatten it for its bed, and is most often displayed by outdoor dogs such as spaniels and other hunting dogs but rarely by toys and other small house dog types.

Marking: Urine marking is an instinctive part of the wolf's communication system and is used to let passersby know that another has just been there. A dog's urine has a peculiar odor that relates to her alone. When Cindy finds a marking spot, she will strain to squirt a drop or two of her urine on that spot. Contrary to popular belief, bitches as well as males mark. Castrated males, and spayed females, mark equally with intact ones. I know of a spayed female Chihuahua that sniffs and marks routinely where other dogs have stained the bottom of posts and rocks.

Olfactory System

Humans are ill equipped to appreciate dogs' scenting ability that allows a dog to detect and follow another animal or object by use of its

A Cocker puppy looking for a nice owner.

olfactory powers. It is a sense that is increased by a special structure in the pharynx called a *vomeronasal organ*, which exists in many mammals to varying degrees. It's observed when you see a dog holding her head high, mouth open, and sometimes making slow licking motions with her tongue rather as if she is tasting the odor.

Tracking and scenting game comes easy to spaniels and other hunting dogs, but is difficult to comprehend by humans because we have a relatively tiny number of olfactory cells compared to the canine (perhaps in the range of 1/40). We also have a propensity to become immune to odors to which we have become accustomed. I'm sure you have delighted at the smell of freshly baked bread on a cool morning in a neighborhood bakery. However, bakery

A brace of Welsh Springers in the field.

workers are so accustomed to this heavenly odor that they can't even smell a loaf coming fresh from their home oven.

A spaniel apparently does not become accustomed to scent of a game bird or other prey. Once learned, each specific scent remains sharp and distinct in Cindy's memory, and even if her concentration is interrupted time after time by other powerful scents, she still remembers that peculiar smell. It is said that a dog can differentiate the scent of a particular person's perspiration from a million others. I don't know how that could be proven but many spaniels and retrievers can discern one single scent out of a myriad of mixtures. That is easily proven by a male dog that detects a female in heat a mile away, by dogs that sniff out contraband at our borders, or unseen explosives on battle fields. That's why Cindy will continue to find and retrieve her feathered quarry, even into old age. Her nose is

the beacon that guides her to familiar people, places, and things in her environment.

Vision

Sight is a wonderful thing and selective breeding has improved upon it. A dog's eyes are among the largest of all pets except cat's. Cindy's field of vision is wider than a human's but her depth perception is less acute. All canines are somewhat farsighted and that makes them masters at detecting motion but less able to perceive stationary objects. It's interesting to note that sighthounds such as Greyhounds, Borzoi, Afghans, and the like are able to follow their prey at extreme speeds using their eyes rather than their untrained scenting abilities. However, Cindy can use her scenting ability to locate a single pheasant in a tightly woven patch of sunflower stalks, even if the bird doesn't move.

Hearing

Canine hearing capacity allows them to perceive 70,000 to 100,000 hertz (sound frequency per second). That enables Cindy to hear sounds that are inaudible to human ears because our range of hearing extends from 16,000 to 20,000 hertz. That fantastic hearing ability is another factor used by a hunting spaniel in her daily work.

Meeting Other Dogs

Cindy is out walking on a leash around the neighborhood and you meet a friend and his new dog that's also on a leash. You stop to chat a few moments and notice that Cindy is taking her time measuring up the friend's dog. First, they hesitate, a few feet apart, sniffing the

These Field Spaniels display the serious curiosity that is typical of the breed.

wind and eyeing each other. They close in, sniff each other, and touch noses. Cindy bounces backward and wags her tail. That breaks the ice and the other dog perks up his ears. You allow her a bit more freedom on the leash and Cindy moves to her newfound friend's side and quickly sniffs his bottom; he responds likewise. They both back off again as if to reevaluate their findings. Cindy is younger than the other dog and she drops to her elbows with her rump in the air, tail wagging, ready to romp.

Your conversation completed, you move off, and Cindy looks over her shoulder several times, each time with her ears raised slightly and her tail wagging. In those few minutes the two dogs have learned all they need to know about each other and each time they meet hereafter they will begin wagging and wriggling as far away as they can see each other. You can depend on their compatibility because Cindy adopted a subordinate position in the pecking order that was almost immediately established because she is younger and a bit smaller and less worldly-wise than the other dog. Oh, were it that simple and honest with people!

Consistency, patience, and gentleness are the keys to a good relationship with your spaniel. Give short, concise commands that Bingo hears plainly and show him what action is expected without harshness. Never be indecisive and never give him a command that can't be accomplished. Above all, don't try to reason with him, and don't expect instant perfection in any endeavors.

Sleeping Environment

While Bingo is still a puppy that requires your attention during the night, put his crate beside your bed. If he begins to whimper or bark, talk to him in a soft voice and don't scold him or feed him. If you think he needs to go outside, take him out. Then return him to his sleeping quarters, pat him on the head, and return to your bed. You may lose a few nights' sleep but once that routine is established his crate will be his bed and you can decide where Bingo is to sleep and put his crate there. Don't allow him to share your bed unless you intend to continue to do so for the next 15 years.

House-training

Pick a spot that can be Bingo's toilet area. It's best situated toward the rear of your back-

A liver and white English Springer Spaniel on guard.

yard and if it's not covered with grass, so much the better. As soon as you pick him up from the breeder take him to that spot and let him sniff around. Take him back there several times the first day, first thing every morning, after each meal, late in the evening, and at the last possible moment before you retire at night. Stay with him in the toilet area until he has defecated and/or urinated. When he does, praise him and tell him what a good dog he is, then pick him up and carry him into the house.

Take him to the toilet area each time he seems restless, squats, or turns in circles, and several times in between just in case. In spite of your self-discipline and efforts he will continue to have occasional accidents unless he's super-intelligent. Don't try to explain that he shouldn't mess on the rug—he's a puppy! He doesn't understand why he shouldn't defecate when he needs to go. If you see him beginning to defecate or urinate in the house, don't shout or startle him. Instead, tell him in a firm

═══ **TIP** ═══

Begging

Spaniels love to eat. We love our canine buddies and tend to reward them to a fault. The result is often a terrible vice known as begging. The best way to train Bingo not to beg is never to allow the habit to become established.

✔ Never feed your spaniel in the kitchen or dining room when you are eating or preparing food.

✔ Never feed him before you and your family eat. It is important for him to learn the pecking order of his human pack.

✔ Always feed him in his own dish, never on your plate or any other dish.

✔ Feed him at specific times each day, no matter how many meals he is being fed.

✔ Never give him food from the table or leftover scraps.

✔ Feed him his regular dog food each meal; dogs do not need changes of their entrées.

✔ Don't experiment with his diet and do not attempt to formulate his diet in your kitchen.

voice "*NO*," pick him up and take him to the toilet area. When he finishes his eliminations, tell him "*Good dog*" and invite him to race you to the house. Patience and praise cost nothing and neither can be neglected.

Cleaning Up

If you find a puddle or a pile of feces after the fact, simply clean up the area with paper towels, then use a good cleaner (not ammonia, as it smells like urine) on the rug or floor. Remember that dogs are attracted to the odor of urine and feces and he will use that same spot again if it isn't cleaned and disinfected very quickly.

When taking him on walks carry a supply of small plastic bags in your pocket or purse and use them to pick up his feces and place it in a proper receptacle.

After he has had all his puppyhood vaccinations, you can take him out of the yard for short walks around the neighborhood. You'll find that treats are no longer necessary because the walk is the reward.

General Grooming

Regular grooming habits will result in a happier dog and a more satisfied owner. If possible, begin Bingo's grooming the first day he's in your home. Place him on a slip-proof mat on a sturdy table of a comfortable height for combing and brushing. Have a friend steady him the first couple of times you groom him and don't let the session last more than ten minutes every two or three days. Professional groomers will gladly take over this duty for you if you can't handle it, but that's not a good plan because regular grooming is a time that you and Bingo should enjoy and is another bonding technique that yields big benefits.

Teeth Care

Start brushing Bingo's teeth while he is still a puppy. Use canine toothpaste and a finger brush or canine toothbrush to clean his teeth for no more than a few minutes every day. His annual physical exam will include a dental examination and you should naturally follow your veterinarian's advice.

Talking to Your Spaniel

Bingo will converse with you, his favorite human, beginning his happy conversation with a woof or certain body language such as searching your face for recognition, wagging his tail, or wriggling all the while. That lets you know he wants to be part of the action. You respond by speaking to him in a soft voice and friendly tone. These conversations are well understood by both parties and often end up with one party getting a face-licking and the other party getting his ears scratched.

Conversely, when you are upset about something you will use a more reserved tone and a curt attitude. These nuances are quickly learned and when you react adversely to his advances he will mope off, mumbling into his beard.

Remember to emanate joy if you wish to see a happy, smiling face whenever Bingo comes into the room. A happy dog is one that will try to please you and that's the attitude you want to cultivate in your spaniel pal.

Punishment

The only punishment you should use is that of ignoring Bingo. If he isn't cooperative, rebels when it comes to your training efforts, and persists on that obstinate tack, simply turn on your curt voice and ignore him. After a few moments of being totally ignored—his overtures going unnoticed, a couple of blunt refusals, and an occasional emphatic "No"—he will probably slink away to think about the

An American Water Spaniel waits for instruction.

A Black and Tan Cocker ready to play.

A Welsh Springer puppy looking for a buddy.

T I P

What Not to Chew

Don't allow your spaniel to chew flimsy rubber or soft squeaky toys because they will soon be destroyed and Bingo may swallow the parts thereof. Those squeakers can cause great mischief in his digestive track. Also, don't let him chew on a shoe, old slipper, or old rag. He's very intelligent but he won't distinguish a brand new Gucci loafer from an old slipper, or your favorite dress shirt from an old rag!

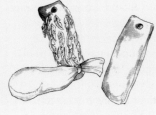

Dummies for training your spaniel to retrieve.

situation. Don't hold a grudge. When he naps for a few minutes and comes running to your side with a toy in his mouth, forgive him and play a few minutes to show him all is well.

Corporal punishment means spanking, swatting, or severely verbally reprimanding Bingo—that is a no-win situation. Dogs are intelligent individuals with long memories when they are positively taught. However, when you momentarily abuse Bingo he will simply think you've lost your mind. He isn't apt to connect your reprimand with his activities of a few moments before. He probably won't think of his own

actions at all but he'll surely remember your change in attitude and that will haunt him in the future.

Suitable Toys

Spaniels are bred to hunt. Use that inherent knowledge and desire to your advantage when you play. Walking Bingo around the neighborhood or in the dog park is an exciting time of his day. He will find every conceivable scent to follow and if you refuse to allow this to happen, you will spoil his fun. After his walk take him to the dog park and toss a ball for him to initiate more vigorous exercise.

Retrieving toys: He will love to give chase and retrieve a tennis ball or to retrieve a feathered dummy. If you really want to ring his chime, sprinkle a couple of drops of bird scent that you can purchase in a sporting goods store or pet supply store on the dummy. If he is a water spaniel and if a safe, accessible lake is nearby, toss the dummy into the water and watch him swim. Go prepared so Bingo doesn't try to retrieve driftwood branches or sticks that might tear his tender mouth or punch him in the eye.

Puppies like to hunt and retrieve as well. Toss a favorite chew toy and after he has retrieved it a few times, have a friend hold him in an another room, hide the toy under a rug or behind a door, then call him into the room and watch his reaction.

The above information and the TIP information are general. Today, certain dogs are taught to differentiate between many different objects by using their highly developed scenting ability, remarkable vision, and advanced word recognition. Results of dogs' newly discovered reasoning powers are being explored and reported almost daily and are highly significant but they aren't usually reported except in special cases under controlled circumstances.

Spaniels and Children

If you have a new baby in your family, don't fail to properly introduce the infant to your spaniel. To avoid jealousy, first introduce the baby to the spaniel by bringing to Bingo a blanket or object that has been in direct contact with the baby. Place the blanket in your spaniel's crate, pet him with it, and make him

English Springers are happy, playful, and full of energy.

very familiar with the scent. Lay it under his food bowl at suppertime and leave it among his bedding. After a day or two of that scent familiarization, bring the baby in and place her on the floor wrapped in her blanket, while you pet and make a fuss over Bingo. Allow him to sniff the infant and lick her feet while you are reassuring your spaniel in the softest voice you can muster. Show your love for both the infant and your pal and end the meeting with a nice treat for Bingo.

Note: Toddlers like to pet, cuddle, and hold furry objects. They are accustomed to pulling the ears of stuffed toys and may try to do the same to poor Bingo. Don't allow tots under the ages of four to five to be in contact with your spaniel in the absence of adult supervision. A particulary tolerant spaniel may allow his ears to be pulled once, but his attitude may change the second time, and he probably will object strenuously.

Children of six to eight generally have been taught sufficient understanding to refrain from dog abuse and can be allowed to take Bingo's leash for walks around the backyard, but not on the street. Nine- or ten-year-olds can usually be trusted to take a well-trained spaniel on walks and both the dog and the kids will appreciate the companionship.

An Irish Water Spaniel with corded coat.

Introducing Another Pet

Introduce Bingo to other pets gradually and on neutral turf.

Other dogs: If the other pet is a dog of the same general size and age as Bingo, simply allow them to meet on a walk while both are restrained by leashes. After the sniffing and overtures are made, encourage them to walk together, exploring the trails, scents, and objects. Next, bring the new dog to Bingo's yard, allow them to sniff through the fence, and later open the gate for the new dog while both are on their respective leashes. After you have evidence of their compatibility, turn them loose and stand back. If they are of a similar age and disposition they're apt to romp, play, and become fast friends. If one is significantly older, larger, or more aggressive, the same technique is used but the preliminary steps are repeated and the process is prolonged.

Cats: If the other pet is a cat or a wild species, take a more conservative course. Put the cat in a crate and set the crate where the two animals can see, smell, and hear each other. After this exposure for several days, put on Bingo's leash and training collar or head harness, trim the cat's front claws, and open the crate. Be sure the cat has an open avenue for escape if that's the course she decides upon. If Bingo ignores the cat when the crate is opened and doesn't try to chase her when she runs away, you can probably trust them together. They might even get to be good friends in the future.

Traveling with Your Spaniel

Many fine hotels and motels from coast to coast welcome pets but traveling by plane or train with a spaniel may be more of a challenge.

A few considerations will facilitate your trip and assure some degree of success with minimal problems.

✔ If traveling by common carrier (train or plane), contact the carrier well in advance and find out the requirements and restrictions that apply.

✔ A motel guide for each of the many chains can be picked up free from a member motel and will tell you what their regulations are regarding pets.

✔ If traveling by auto and crossing state lines take Bingo to his hometown veterinarian a week before travel for a physical checkup, renewal of his vaccinations, and a health certificate. A health certificate isn't required by most states but it will save you a lot of explaining if a local authority wants any health information about your dog or if it becomes lost in a strange town.

✔ Ask your veterinarian if there are any diseases in areas to which you are traveling that Bingo isn't exposed to in your hometown (for instance, Lyme disease or coccidioidomycosis). Listen to her answer and follow her advice very carefully.

✔ If Bingo doesn't already have a crate, now is the time to purchase one. Also buy a water pan that clamps to the inside of the crate. Crate travel is safer for him in the car and serves as a handy bed in motels.

✔ Beware of heatstroke. Put a thermometer in his traveling crate and check its temperature at every stop. The temperature within the crate in the backseat can become a health risk even if it is cool in the front seat.

This Champion Sussex is proudly showing his winning ways.

✔ Don't forget to take Bingo for walks at rest stops. Try to stop at least every two hours for your own safety as well as Bingo's. Check his water dish at every stop and carry bottled water for him to drink.

✔ Pack some of his normal food for the trip. Changes in diet may initiate diarrhea.

✔ Take along two or three large spare towels for bedding and to clean up water spills inside his crate.

✔ Take a big supply of small plastic bags to clean up his droppings on walks.

✔ Take along a first aid kit for yourself and Bingo because it's better to be prepared than to have a day of the trip spoiled by some minor accident.

Normally Bingo will hardly ever need a bath but when he rolls in something nasty or plays in the mud after a rain, it may be necessary. Prepare everything in advance so as to make the bathing process as painless and swift as possible. Have the following items ready:

✔ Sturdy table of a convenient height
✔ Bathtub or utility sink that will accommodate the spaniel
✔ Metal comb with blunt teeth
✔ Mat splitter
✔ Nail trimmer
✔ Pair of blunt scissors
✔ Rubberized plastic bathmat
✔ Bottle of canine shampoo
✔ Bottle of 2 percent hydrogen peroxide
✔ Shower hose that adapts to the faucet
✔ Tube of sterile petrolatum ointment
✔ Soft sponge
✔ Handful of cotton balls
✔ Several large terrycloth towels
✔ Quiet electric hair dryer with a low or warm setting

Mats

Stand Bingo on a sturdy table and comb his coat thoroughly. If you find mats, first use a mat splitter then continue combing until his guard coat is clean and free of any mats or tangles. If tangles persist and are easily isolated from his skin, cut them out with scissors. Be particularly careful when splitting mats between toes or pads or on the fringe of his ears. If necessary, employ the assistance of a friend or family member to hold your spaniel to assure that you don't cut the web between his toes or his ear margins.

If Bingo has stepped in gum or tar it will undoubtedly become matted into the long hair between his pads. Either split the matted hair with the mat splitter, cut it out with scissors, or rub petrolatum jelly into the gum until it loosens and then wash it out of the hair with soap and water.

Nails

Turn his feet upside down one at a time. Push the hair away from his toenails and you will see that each toenail is somewhat hollow and V-shaped. Using a sharp canine nail trimmer of the scissor variety, begin at the tip of the nail and progressively snip off tiny slices of the nail until the cross-section of the nail is shaped like a circle with a notch in the bottom instead of V-shaped.

Face and Eyes

Clean Bingo's face with a water-dampened soft sponge.

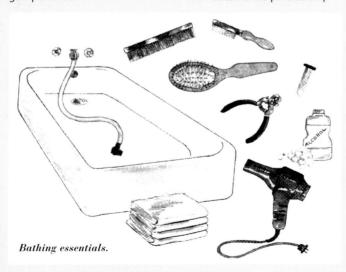

Bathing essentials.

Use no shampoo near his eyes. Squeeze about a ¼-inch (6-mm) ribbon of petrolatum jelly onto the cornea of each eye. This will protect the sensitive corneas from soap.

Ears

Use a cotton ball moistened with 2 percent hydrogen peroxide or other proven ear wash to clean the dirt and wax from his external ear canals. Do not push a cotton swab into his ear canal where your finger can't reach. Put a dry cotton ball in each of his ears and carefully push them down into the canals, but not so far as to be difficult to reach with your fingers. Make note of evidence of scratching or redness of his ear canals, or a foul odor that emanates from them. If either of those signs is discovered, take him to your veterinarian as soon as you can make an appointment. Smelly ears are a possible sign of ear mites or bacterial ear canal infection.

The Tub

1. Place the rubber mat into the tub or sink so he won't slip and fall.

2. Fill the tub with tepid water to about the level of his belly.

3. Stand Bingo in the tub.

4. Scoop up handfuls of water and wet his head and ears. Using the sprayer hose, soak his legs, shoulders, belly, tail, and back. Although you have protected his eyes and ears, try your best not to splash his face with water because most spaniels that love to swim and dive still hate to have soapy bathwater splashed in their faces.

5. When his coat is thoroughly saturated, squeeze out small portions of shampoo, work-

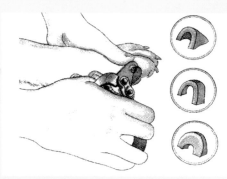

Good technique for trimming nails.

ing each into the coat of his belly, feet, legs, neck, ears, and tail.

6. Lather his ears and gently squeeze the soap and water from them. Leave his face as nearly dry as possible.

7. Turn on the warm water and press the hand-held shower nozzle close to his back, legs, and abdomen until his coat is rinsed free of shampoo.

8. Rinse his ears the same way, squeezing the excess water from them.

9. Drain the water from the tub and fill it again to the same level with warm rinse water.

10. Repeat the rinsing action with the hand-held shower nozzle pressed against his coat.

11. Drain the tub and squeeze as much water as possible from his coat.

12. Towel him as dry as possible. Take him from the tub and stand him on a towel on the floor or table. Remove the cotton earplugs.

13. Finish drying him with a hand-held hair dryer. If the weather is cool, be sure he stays indoors until all his heavy coat is totally dry. If necessary, confine him to his crate.

SPANIEL NUTRITION

Feed Bingo a balanced and nutritious diet. The best food for him is one of the premium-quality, dry dog foods. It can be fed by itself or in combination with a small amount of premium canned food to increase palatability. It is foolish to try to formulate a food in your kitchen that compares favorably with a commercial, premium canine diet. It is equally foolish to offer your spaniel a cheap, inadequate food, then add a vitamin-mineral supplement in an effort to balance it.

What Is AAFCO?

The American Association of Feed Control Officials consists of representatives from each state. This organization regulates dog food labels such as *Complete and Balanced*. The AAFCO label on a dog food means it is proven to be complete and balanced by feeding trials. Dog foods typically are labeled for puppies, youths, adults, and working adults.

Dietary Essentials

Water

Water is an important element that is often overlooked when discussing diet. Bingo is an active spaniel and he needs lots of fresh drinking water. Dehydration and its many complica-

A Field Spaniel, beautiful, but ready to work.

tions are commonly seen in hot weather and a spaniel's heavy coat means he needs even more water than short-coated individuals. He should never be without a source of fresh drinking water.

Protein

All protein has much the same dietary value, whether it originates from animal tissues or vegetables. The palatability and bioavailability of animal-origin protein is greater than that of plant protein but both types are constructed from identical amino acids. Ten amino acids are essential for canine life, and their deficiency can cause many problems such as dull coat, immune deficiency, retarded growth, retarded muscular development, weight loss, and if not corrected, death. A diet containing about 18 percent protein that includes all essential amino acids is advised for most adult spaniels.

A Cocker Spaniel in full show coat stands ready to get to the ring.

the essential fatty acids. Animal fats are more palatable than those of vegetable sources but vegetables cost less so naturally they're found in greater quantity in dog foods. Diets containing about 5 percent fat are adequate for Bingo; a higher level shouldn't be fed unless you check first with your veterinarian.

Carbohydrates

Carbohydrate (starch) is the cheapest ingredient in dog foods and is derived from plant sources. Your spaniel doesn't actually require carbohydrates for life but they are used in his food in proper ratio with protein and fat to supply necessary calories.

Vitamins and Minerals

AAFCO recommends 11 vitamins that should be in all dog foods. Vitamin C isn't among those essential vitamins because the canine has the ability to manufacture sufficient quantities of vitamin C without external sources. If you feed Bingo a premium dog food, it will meet all his vitamin needs.

Have your veterinarian check Bingo if his coat appears dry or if he seems to lack energy. Use a dietary supplement if prescribed, but don't go overboard. Some vitamins can be dangerous in high doses and any vitamin supplement must be balanced with the diet to be effective. For instance, high doses of vitamin A are toxic, vitamin D must be given with certain levels of calcium and phosphorus, and fat-soluble vitamins such as A, E, and K must be given with sufficient fatty acids to be absorbed.

Twelve minerals in specific quantities are required by dogs and those minerals generally can be found in any good food. Calcium and

Puppy diets should contain more high-quality protein; up to 25 percent is preferable in a puppy's diet. Old dogs with kidney compromise should be fed differently and their diets usually contain less protein of a higher bioavailability to minimize the stress on old kidneys.

Fat

Fat can also be derived from animal or vegetable sources and both types contain all of

This photo of seven English Cocker puppies took hours to pose.

phosphorus should be provided in a ratio of 1.2 parts calcium to 1 part phosphorus to provide correct balance and the sources of calcium and phosphorus are also important.

Working spaniels, those in strenuous training, or those that are subjected to temperature extremes should be fed special diets and/or dietary supplements. Consult with your veterinarian and choose a premium diet that is specifically formulated to supply proper levels of nutrients.

Puppies' vitamin and mineral requirements are important but they are supplied by feeding premium puppy foods in the quantities prescribed. Never add calcium, bone meal, or other minerals to Bingo's diet—too much calcium in a puppy's food may cause irreversible damage.

Dog Food Types

Hundreds of brands, but only three different types, of dog food are found on the supermar-

ket shelves. Those types are semimoist, canned, and dry.

Semimoist foods are soft and palatable. They are usually marketed in plastic bags so the owner can see the product that appears to be chunks of meat. That type appeals to owners who choose by appearance alone. The product's principal disadvantage is cost but often nutritional problems are associated with the quantity of sugar and other carbohydrates that are contained in the product. Other problems are the chemical preservatives that keep the product looking meaty in the little plastic bag. Preservatives often cause dogs to drink great quantities of water, which leads to frequent urination. Some of these products cause allergic reactions as well. All these reasons seem to rule out this dog food type for Bingo.

Canned foods are very expensive because in these you are buying more than 60 percent water. Canned foods may also contain an insufficient quantity of roughage for proper

TIP

Table Scraps

Your spaniel deserves the best food that you can buy, but actually it isn't very expensive if you know what is available, can read the dog food labels, and understand what they mean. It's a bad idea to feed Bingo your leftovers. You might get by and he may be happy but you'll never see his best if you're shorting him on balanced nutrition. A few treats of cooked meat are okay as long as they are fed in tiny quantities and as long as he is also fed a sound regular diet.

A Cocker cleaning the last bit from the bowl.

digestion and some preservatives are used that may cause Bingo to urinate more frequently than necessary. Be aware that everything inside the can isn't necessarily of the greatest quality and often includes a minimal amount of meat.

Dry dog foods are usually the best choice for most dogs. The price is usually more in line with the nutrition delivered, and balanced nutrition can be assured by feeding a premium dry food alone. That makes sense. Chances are you won't need special flavoring to convince Bingo to eat heartily and you won't need supplements or additions of any kind to assure balance. In case he tells you that the food you chose is less than palatable, try mixing a bit of chicken or beef bouillon or meat flavoring to the warm water you use to moisten the food, then try a different brand of premium food the next time you buy a bag.

Dog Food Labels

All labels are legal documents and should be read carefully if you want to use them correctly.

✔ If a label tells consumers that it is *complete*, that means for nutrition of normal dogs; nothing else needs to be added.

✔ If it reads *complementary*, that means it should be combined with a supplement.

✔ Ingredients are listed in order of their quantity. If soy flour is the first ingredient listed, it is in greater quantity than any other. If the first ingredient listed is lamb, that means more lamb is in the food than any other ingredient. If beef is listed last (for instance, after all vitamins and minerals), you can bet the farm that not much beef is found within.

✔ If a label states that the food meets the recommendations of the NRC (National

The diet of a hard-charging hunting dog will vary in energy requirements from that of an average house pet.

Research Council), you know only that the dog food is adequate for maintenance and doesn't address stress conditions. In other words, the food may be inadequate for growth, training, work, and so forth.

✔ If a label states that the food has passed the AAFCO feeding trials for a dog's entire life cycle, you can be assured that the food contains the right amount of bioavailable nutrients for growth, maintenance, and normal work.

Labels rarely reveal the bioavailability of ingredients. That is highly significant because if a food has a certain level of a needed nutrient but the ingredient isn't in a form that's available to the dog through normal digestion, it might as well be absent. Labels should list the source of protein contained, and whether it is of animal or vegetable origin. If any of your questions are unanswered on the label, call the manufacturer on the toll-free number fur-

nished. Your veterinarian will also give you good advice and you can certainly inquire about canine requirements on the Internet. Of course, please remember that not everything that's seen on the Internet is perfect or even reasonable; the credentials of the writer might be no better than your own.

Treats

Treats are a fact of life. Bingo needs a certain amount of treats! That may be a little overstated but treats do enhance training, obedience to commands, and are important just because you love your companion. Use your head and treats won't be a problem. Give Bingo a low-calorie treat biscuit or a tiny piece of baked liver or an equally small bit of cooked chicken or beef. Keep track of the quantity you are feeding daily and if it is more than a dozen tidbits rethink your program.

A Welsh Springer stands groomed to perfection and ready to enter the show ring.

Overfeeding

Don't feed your spaniel all he wants or all he will eat at one time. It's perfectly normal for Bingo to beg for another bite after he's finished eating his meal. Obesity is a killer of dogs. If you aren't sure that your spaniel is about the right weight, palpate his rib cage. You should be able to feel his ribs easily through the fat layer. If they stand out like a picket fence, increase his daily food intake. If his ribs are buried beneath the fat layer, he's too fat and you're feeding him too much.

This Field Spaniel has a serious expression that masks his mischieviousness.

You can also weigh him. Pick him up and step on a bathroom scale. Subtract your weight and the rest is Bingo. If you do that after a visit to your veterinarian, who told you that Bingo was in perfect condition, you should be able to maintain his weight within a pound or two. If he's in heavy training or working hard, increase his daily ration by adding another small meal to his schedule. Anytime you aren't comfortable with Bingo's looks, feel, or performance, ask your veterinarian or Bingo's breeder to evaluate his condition.

Feeding Schedule

When you picked up Bingo from his breeder you received instructions about the amount he should be fed and the frequency of his meals. Generally, the recommendation is for three meals per day of a premium-quality puppy food. That is good advice if he is a healthy puppy, getting a healthy amount of daily exercise, and is free of internal parasites. Your breeder or veterinarian or your common sense should have told you to gradually increase the quantity of each meal as he grows.

When he reaches six months of age, his meals can be reduced to two per day, maintaining the amount previously fed in three meals. The daily ration should continue to be increased slowly until he matures. If he's a small spaniel, such as a Cocker, he will mature a little earlier than his larger cousins. In any case, when he reaches maturity his daily ration needs no further increases unless he's under some type of stress. In case he is working in obedience training, gundog training, retriever

A Black and Tan Field Spaniel.

===== TIP =====

What Not to Feed
✔ Meat scraps will destroy the nutritional balance of a dog food.
✔ Milk or ice cream will cause diarrhea in many dogs.
✔ Raw eggs will interfere with his absorption of biotin, a B-complex vitamin.
✔ Lard, fat, or vegetable oils may cause diarrhea and will interfere with nutritional balance.
✔ Cooked bones of any kind may splinter and cause mouth or gut damage.
✔ Table scraps of all kinds will interfere with the nutritional balance of dog food.

training, or any other stress situation, he might require more nutrition than during his growth phase. Continue to monitor his weight and as he finishes training sessions and begins to relax as an adult member of the family, he will require fewer calories per day than he has during the previous, more active, stages of life.

TRAINING AND CARE OF YOUR SPANIEL

A domestic dog has many instincts similar to its progenitors, the wolves. However a domestic dog's intelligence is greater than the sum of its hereditary, instinctive knowledge and behavior because for eons dogs have been selectively bred for specific purposes. Cindy's hereditary traits plus her long ancestry as a spaniel bred for a specific purpose, are added to her experiences throughout life and make up her total knowledge and intelligence.

Human Influence

Developmental knowledge can be thwarted by human indifference and neglect and it can be enhanced by training and trust. A perfect example is found in potential guide dog breeds such as German Shepherd Dogs, Labrador Retrievers, and Golden Retrievers. Guide dog candidates are instinctively no more intelligent than others. Those dogs are individually selected because of their trainability, which may be defined as a dog's desire to focus on its trainer, to listen to commands, and interpret the trainer's actions and responses. Cindy's trainability is related to her more recent ancestry than her wolf progenitors.

An Irish Water Spaniel dressed for cold water.

A Matter of Trust

Hold a family powwow. Ask everyone in the group to not issue Cindy any training commands until you have told them that it's okay. A puppy is terribly confused if two or three people use different commands and expect a uniform response. The rule should be that only one person is responsible for training. After the dog has mastered a particular command, anyone that she knows can give it, but it must always be given in the same way it was taught.

The reason for establishing a mutual trust with your spaniel is to create a happy, loving, obedient, and predictable pet, one that you are always proud of. Being an intelligent spaniel, Cindy will quickly bond with her owner if she is always treated fairly. Bonding is a mutual trust

The beautiful flowing coat of this English Springer will pay off in the show ring.

and the key word is *mutual.* From the time of her puppyhood she looks to her favorite human (you) for everything she needs in life. If she finds what she needs, she will continue to focus on you and will trust you in the future. If she trusts you she will want to please you and the more she pleases you, the more you can trust her. She will become focused and obedient without even realizing what obedience means.

Mistakes

Spaniels are forgiving individuals that can overlook infrequent little mistakes that you make, and you must also forgive Cindy's mistakes. Trust may be severely damaged or even lost if she is neglected or if she's physically or mentally abused. Likewise, confidence in her human leader wanes if she receives commands that are confusing or complex or physically

impossible to perform. Irreparable damage will be caused if her training is pushed too fast and she's not given time to fully understand what is desired of her. Under any of those circumstances Cindy will become discouraged and gradually she will stop trying to please her owner.

Your job as her trainer is to assure her daily that she's the most intelligent, clever, and willing dog in the world. That foundation should begin when she first arrives in your home. All training discussed at this time should be done within the confines of your house or fenced backyard.

Command as She Does

Whenever possible use the *command as she does* technique. This means you pick a time when Cindy is already doing your bidding, then give the command and she will connect it with whatever she is doing. For instance: on the first day in your yard when she wanders off, squat down, call her name—*Cindy!*—hesitate, and when she looks around and sees you at her level she will begin to run toward you. At that second, give her the command "*Come.*" Or, when it's dinnertime and you see her in the yard, say "*Cindy!*," hesitate, then say "*Come!*" When she smells her dinner, sees her bowl in your hand, and hears your call, her response is immediate. She has painlessly learned both her name and the *recall (come)* command. When she arrives, set the bowl down, tell her "*Good dog,*" and stroke her head. Within a day she will come to you each time she hears her name and the *come* command. The reward she

Rules for Training

1. Pick a spot that's secure, such as your backyard. Beginner training should always be taught without an audience and without any disturbances.

2. Never, *ever* scold, discipline, or punish your spaniel after calling her to your side.

3. Always first give a command that she has already mastered, then proceed to the new command you are teaching.

4. Always make the training sessions brief, never more than five or ten minutes.

5. Never introduce more than one command per session.

6. Never give complex commands; her name and a single word are sufficient.

7. Always have a physical encouragement in mind before you start the session; for instance, prepare to put your hand on her rump when teaching her to sit.

8. Always train her to respond to commands in a consistent manner. Stop, think, and perform, without hesitation.

9. In the beginning always train with treats. Later you can probably rely on other rewards but spaniels like to nibble and will learn faster if a treat is the reward.

10. If she is confused, probably it's because the command isn't clear.

11. If she doesn't seem to understand a command, stop trying to teach it for a week. During that time, consult a training manual or discuss the problem with a trainer, and rethink what you're asking of your dog, then try it again.

12. If for any reason Cindy is unable or unwilling to perform a command, don't lose your patience. Never lose your temper or composure and always end all training sessions with a command you're sure she can perform.

receives when the command is executed may be your soft-spoken words of praise, a couple of loving strokes, a game of ball, a treat from your fingers, or any other act that she enjoys.

Refusal

In the unlikely case that Cindy refuses to come to you every time you call her, the fault may not be hers—maybe you've broken the trust by failing to give her a reward. Reward is very important to a beginner puppy. Perhaps

someone in the family has called her, then grabbed her up and scolded her or punished her. Maybe a child has repeated the *recall* command without reason, time and again, and without giving a reward and without actually doing something with her.

If any of those things happen, explain to everyone the proper sequence of commands, caution them how to use this very important command and begin all over again. She will relearn what she once had mastered but it may

An Irish Water Spaniel taking a jump in an obedience trial.

take longer next time. If a stubborn streak has crept into the entire *recall*-training program, fasten a long lightweight nylon cord to her collar. Allow her to wander away, then say "*Cindy, come*" and at that instant, gently and firmly pull her toward you. When she reaches your side, reward her and repeat the exercise two or three times, then wait until tomorrow and see if you should again employ the cord.

Every time Cindy runs to your side, whether or not you've called her, reward her with praise and stroking. If she runs away from you, use the *recall* command and if she ignores you, ignore her. That's right, simply turn your back and trot away without repeating the command. Invariably she will forget why she was running

away, and begin chasing you. After a few steps, stop, turn to her, praise her as she approaches, and stroke her head lovingly. That is the time to also give her a treat to reinforce the obedience.

Collar and Leash Training

Collars are resented by all puppies the first few times they are employed but Cindy will learn quickly that a collar has positive benefits, because all puppies love their owners and love to be taken for walks.

1. Begin training Cindy to wear a collar and walk on a leash as soon as she is comfortable in your home. Buckle her nylon or leather collar in place. She will scratch at it, whimper, and fuss a few minutes but ignore her discontent, and within a short time she will forget it, especially if it's suppertime or if you toss her ball a few times. Take the collar off at night the first week. After that time you can leave it in place 24 hours a day except when you are training her; at those times use the training collar.

2. The second or third day after you buckle her collar on, tie a shoelace to the collar and let Cindy drag it around the yard a while. An occasional puppy will not quickly accept the string attached to the collar, in which case you should tempt her with her favorite treats. Pinch off a tiny piece of meat and show it to her, letting her smell it as you back away from her. Chances are she'll follow you anywhere to get the treat and before you know it, she's dragging the shoestring all around the yard.

3. After she no longer pays any attention to it, pick up the end of the string and follow her as she moves around. She will soon reach the conclusion that the string is staying, that it isn't trying to hurt her, and when you pick up the end you're not going to pull her around. After a few days of following her, exchange the shoestring for a lightweight leash. Pick up the loop of the leash and show her a treat in your other hand. Hold it in front of her nose for a while, then give it to her and praise her. Within a few days, walking on a leash will be second nature to her. Take her for a walk around the yard several times daily and when she has performed nicely on the leash, praise, treat, and release her.

Simple Training Commands

Cindy has learned her name and the critical *recall* command without realizing it. A few

A Field Spaniel that has been groomed for the show ring.

other commands are described below that will further her education. Remember to always use her name first, then a single-word command. First say her name. That's to get her undivided attention and her focus on you and what you are to ask of her.

No

No is a command that leads the list of necessary commands for a puppy to learn. *No* is not a negotiable suggestion. It is a command and it always means to stop, think about where you are and what you are doing, and stop doing it. Immediately! Anytime Cindy gets on the furniture, tell her, "*Cindy, NO!*" Use a special voice that leaves no doubt as to your meaning. Say "*No*" when Cindy chases the cat, begs at the table, chews the furniture, or urinates on the rug. *No* is not punishment, it is not a reprimand, it is simply a command that she must learn and

An Irish Water Spaniel's thick coat protects it from the cold water in which it works.

respect early in life. After issuing the command, reinforce it by physically removing the object she was chewing, plucking her from the sofa, or carrying her outside to the toilet area.

Sit

Sit is logically the next command to teach. *Sit* is usually simple, easily taught, and can begin as soon as Cindy knows her name.

✔ Before you start, put a supply of treats in your pocket and stand Cindy before you, with her rump to a wall.

✔ Kneel down in front of your student and tell her *"Cindy, sit."*

✔ Immediately show her a tidbit in front of and near her muzzle but don't let her take it.

✔ Begin moving it back, about 2 inches (5.1 cm) above her head. When it reaches her eyes she will find it necessary to either back up or sit. At that time, raise the treat an inch (2.5 cm) and she will sit. If necessary, you may place your other hand on her rump and exert gentle pressure, which will further encourage her to sit, but usually that's not necessary.

✔ The instant her bottom rests on the floor, give her the treat, praise her, and pet her for a few seconds, then give her the release command, *"Okay."*

✔ As you say "*Okay*" stand up and move back. Let her wander around for a few minutes then give her the *recall* command, "*Cindy, come.*"

✔ When she arrives, place her as before, kneel, and repeat the *sit* command.

✔ After she's performed satisfactorily a few times, the session is over. After a day or two of repeated sitting in the same sequence of commands, give her the *sit* command without calling her to you. That should tell you whether or not she really has the hang of it.

Down

Down is another command that she should learn.

✔ To begin, give her the *recall* and *sit* commands.

✔ When she is sitting, give her the command, "*Cindy, down.*"

✔ Hold her reward under her nose and move it downward until it is literally touching the floor. She will follow it downward and end up lying on her belly. If she does, give her the treat, praise her, and after a few seconds, release her with the *okay* command.

✔ It is rarely necessary to give physical encouragement but if necessary, place your hand on her withers (shoulder blades) and gently push downward.

Stay

Stay is a bit more complicated for Cindy to understand but the technique is about the same.

✔ First call her to you and give her the *sit* and *down* commands.

✔ When she is lying before you, show her the palm of your hand with your fingers pointing upward and say, "*Cindy, stay.*"

✔ Hold your position in front of her the first few times and keep repeating softly and slowly, "*staaay, staaay.*"

✔ Then give her the treat and release her with a snappy "*Okay.*"

✔ Repeat this exercise a few times, resting a few minutes in between. Repeat it the second day except when she's down and staying, take a step backward, still facing her, with your hand signal still being used. The next day, step back several paces; all else the same.

✔ Repeat daily with the length of *stay* time and your distance being increased each day. When she is staying for 30 seconds without rising, turn and walk a few steps with your back to her. Then return to her, give the treat, praise, and release her.

A Welsh Springer puppy trying her hand at hunting.

TIP

To Obtain Information

Space doesn't allow detailed information about the AKC Spaniel Tests and Trials (page 70). If you are interested in having your spaniel hunt-tested, or if you are interested in competing in AKC spaniel field trials, talk to your local spaniel club secretary or the secretary of the specialty club formed by your particular breed. Tests and trials are run in virtually every part of the country and can be entered by any AKC registered spaniel.

Sit-Stay

Sit-stay command is taught the same way except that she stays in the sitting position. It usually comes naturally after she has recognized the rules of the game and is obeying the *down* and *stay* commands.

Walk On

Walk on is another command that is important to use when taking a walk in your yard or around the neighborhood. If you stop to chat with a neighbor, give Cindy the *sit* command and when you're finished talking, give the command "*Cindy, walk on.*" At the same time, begin to move ahead and she will respond naturally to the command.

Soon you will see that she is focusing on you all the time you are playing teacher and the more she focuses, the better she will respond.

Heel

Heel is an obedience command that doesn't come naturally because Cindy likes to walk ahead of her human companion. Don't even begin teaching this discipline before she is six or more months old. If she isn't likely to compete in obedience, it isn't necessary to teach her to *heel* in the strict AKC obedience trial manner.

✔ Use her training collar to teach this command. Drop the chain training collar through one of its rings so it forms a noose. Then attach the leash snap to the training ring and place the collar on Cindy so that the end of the collar that is attached to the leash comes up the left side of her neck and crosses from left to right over the top of her neck (see illustration on page 32).

Modern obedience training developed in large part from the disciplines of the hunting field.

✔ When it is necessary to correct Cindy's action, the collar is given a gentle tug, then released. If the training collar is placed correctly, it snugs up immediately, releases quickly, and can't possibly injure her throat or internal structures of her neck. If the training collar is too big, it will not close quickly enough to be effective.

✔ Begin with Cindy on your left, her nose even with your knee or shin.

✔ Run her leash through your left hand and hold it with your right. Give her the *sit* command, hesitate a moment, step off with your right foot, tell her "*Cindy, heel,*" and walk at a normal pace.

In obedience trials Cindy will be required to maintain her same position as you slow down, speed up, and turn. When you stop, she must be taught to sit in the *heeling* position. Heeling is not the spaniel's favorite exercise and some never get it right without hours of patient training. Never expect to convince Cindy that her walks around the neighborhood should be done with her at heel.

Fetch

Fetching or retrieving is a natural discipline for most spaniels and is one of the easiest to teach to a puppy, but you must instill in your Spaniel the difference between retrieving and playing catch. To teach her to retrieve, use a special scented dummy, maybe even one with feathers on it. You can buy a variety of these dummies at sports stores. A dummy should always be used instead of a ball that Cindy carries around and begs to have someone throw for her.

✔ Begin retriever training in your backyard. Have a friend hold Cindy by her web collar with a long lightweight nylon line attached.

An American Water Spaniel Champion showing her stuff.

✔ Show her the dummy and let her smell it. Then toss it straight out in front of you about 20 or 30 feet (6.1–9 m) away. Tell her "*Mark*" as it hits the ground.

✔ Then tell her, "*Cindy, fetch,*" at which time your friend will turn her loose. Hold onto the cord. She will undoubtedly race to the dummy and pick it up.

✔ Tell her "*Cindy, come,*" and take up the slack in the line. She will probably bring the dummy to you but if she decides to take off in the other direction, you can control her escape by pulling the line, thus leading her directly to you.

✔ When she arrives in front of you, tell her "*Give*" and at the same time offer her a treat and praise her when she drops the dummy at your feet.

✔ After she has conquered the retrieving exercise, try a few variations: Let her smell the dummy, then hold her and shield her from your friend who is dragging the dummy away and hiding it in tall grass or bushes somewhere within 20 or 30 feet (6.1–9 m) of her. Then throw the dummy into tall grass, brush, or any other heavy cover. She will soon realize that this seeking, finding, and retrieving discipline has a fuller meaning than just chasing a toy or ball and she will try harder and use her scenting powers more than her vision.

✔ After she gets the hang of the exercise she will not require the long line and will bring the dummy to your hand every time it's thrown.

✔ Put the dummy away and out of her reach when the training session is over. Never let her play with it, run away with it, and especially don't allow her to chew on it. Natural retrievers such as spaniels can get worn out or bored with any training, even retrieving scented and feathered dummies. Don't overdo it! Eight or ten retrieves at a single session is enough!

Take Me Out to the Ball Game

Playing ball is a different game altogether, in which you or your family can initiate Cindy's exercise and have a good time running and playing keep away, who's got the ball, and hide and seek. It really doesn't matter what is happening to the ball if everyone is having fun but it's best to put the tennis ball out of her reach when the games are over. Give her safe rawhide bones to chew on, not tennis balls.

AKC Spaniel Events

The American Kennel Club sponsors many competitive and sporting events that attract intelligent dogs and their owners. Most of these events invite participation by all pure-bred dogs, but two are designed exclusively for spaniels and are discussed briefly.

Spaniel Hunting Tests

A request for an AKC-sponsored Spaniel Gun Dog Qualification Test was put to the AKC in the mid-1980s, was pursued by an advisory committee, and became a reality on July 13, 1988 in Pescardero, California when the first Spaniel Hunting Test was run. A Spaniel Hunting Test is open to all AKC-registrable breeds of Flushing Spaniels six months old or over. The Flushing Spaniel breeds included for participation are Clumber Spaniels, Cocker Spaniels, English Cocker Spaniels, English Springer Spaniels, Field Spaniels, Sussex Spaniels, and Welsh Springer Spaniels. In other words, all of the spaniels covered by this book except the Irish Water Spaniel and American Water Spaniel are eligible.

The tests are overseen by qualified judges and are meant to test the proficiency of a spaniel at searching for feathered game within gunshot range of the handler, flushing birds into the air, and retrieving downed birds on command of the handler. These tests are not competitive and are not scored by points, but are a test to gauge the dog's natural abilities during the demands of actual hunting conditions.

Spaniel Field Trials

The purpose of spaniel field trials is to demonstrate the performance of a trained spaniel in the field. It differs from a hunting test in that spaniels running in a field trial are competitively judged and awards are given to those that best perform the various parts of the trial. Scoring is by points, and titles are established accordingly. The performance demanded doesn't differ much from a day's shooting except that in a trial, each dog should do work in a nearly perfect way.

1. The spaniel walks at heel or on leash until the handler is ordered to seek game by the judge. At that time the spaniel must seek out

A Cocker Spaniel flying over agility trial jump.

game birds, always working within gunshot distance in front of the handler.

2. She must, without urging, flush the birds into the air, mark the downed ones, and upon command of her handler (when instructed by the judge), retrieve the birds to her handler's hand.

3. Then she should sit at the handler's *hup* command and await further commands.

Trial participants are scored on the perfection displayed on each of the phases of the trial. The difference between high scoring and barely passing lies in the manner and attitude of the spaniel. She must obey all commands quickly and must flush all game in the territory designated, show intensity and courage when going into cover, mark the fallen birds, and retrieve them speedily and tenderly without excessive mouthing.

Other Competitions

Agility Trials and Fly Ball are other AKC competitions that spaniel owners love to watch, and maybe Cindy is suited for one or more of them. Frisbee contests are a riot to watch and more fun to participate in. They aren't governed by the AKC but are held in virtually every part of the country. Freestyle Dancing is another endeavor that you might like—it is amply explained on the Internet with associations and rules that apply.

If you wish to educate yourself further on any of these activities, visit the Internet's many references. Keep in mind that not all of the various papers published on the Internet are written by experts. Don't trust some individual's information. Go to state or national clubs or to the AKC for reliable information.

Well means a satisfactory state of health or physical condition, or being able to perform favorably and comfortably— the condition or state of being healthy or sound. By definition, sick is the opposite. It means being unwell. It refers to suffering from disease, being in poor condition, being physically or mentally impaired.

Choosing a Veterinarian

Before discussing Bingo's health, another subject springs to mind and that is: How does a new spaniel owner find a reputable veterinarian to oversee Bingo's health? You want a practitioner who knows spaniels, one who understands hunting dogs, whether or not you intend to train your dog to retrieve game. Bingo deserves a knowledgeable, caring doctor who has a wonderful bedside manner, is loaded with advice, and freely dispenses it. This veterinarian must be trustworthy to examine and prescribe for Bingo's illnesses, perform surgery, and advise you about Bingo's preventive medicine program. An up-to-date knowledge of modern drugs and equipment is mandatory, as is the ability and knowledge of the latest diagnostic techniques.

✔ Take your time. Don't hurry your decision. Most animal hospitals are pleased to offer new

This Sussex Spaniel displays a sturdy, strong body that adds to its beauty.

dog owners a free visual examination the day the new puppy is picked up.

✔ Visit more than one clinic and talk to both the technical staff and the veterinarian.

✔ Observe the veterinarian's ability and attitude as she examines Bingo.

✔ Listen carefully to what she has to say and how she explains what is needed. See if she demonstrates patience and knowledge and watch Bingo as her skilled hands handle him.

✔ Ask questions and notice whether they receive careful consideration before they are answered.

✔ Note whether or not the examination is rushed or an assistant is called to help handle Bingo, and whether your questions are ignored or don't receive full attention.

✔ Ask about fees and expect to receive answers quickly and perhaps a copy of a fee schedule.

✔ Make an appointment for further visits only if you and Bingo agree that this is the proper clinic and clinician for you.

Normal Signs of a Healthy Spaniel

Eye Appearance	Corneas clear and moist. Blood vessels that are tiny and confined to the sclera (white of the eyeball). White of the eyes bright and without discoloration.
Mucous Membranes	Gums, tongue, underside of lips should be bright pink and moist.
Coat	Rich and glossy, feels slightly oily to the touch, not dry or brittle.
Gait	Walks, trots, and runs easily without lameness or hesitation. Holds both head and tail in a normal manner.
Attitude	Acts bright and alert. Wags his tail in expectation when you speak. Doesn't try to hide. Responds happily to his toys or training dummies. Doesn't slink about.
Appetite	Eats his normal meals in a timely manner. Doesn't vomit or work his food around with his tongue before swallowing.
Water Consumption	Drinks about the same each day unless outside temperatures are high or exercise is more prolonged. Daily consumption can be measured by putting a known amount in his bowl, filling it when empty and recording the amount he drinks in a specific time period.
Stools	Normally formed and colored, without blood or mucus, passed without undue straining.
Urine	Bright light-yellow color, in normal quantities without blood or mucus visible.
Temperature	101.5°F (38°C) is the average rectal temperature taken with a digital or standard glass thermometer; may vary by one degree higher or lower.
Respiration	10 to 20 per minute, taken when Bingo is resting; will raise with exercise or excitement.
Respiratory Character	Even and deep, taken when Bingo is resting and not panting.
Pulse Rate	70 to 80 per minute taken by pressing a finger inside Bingo's thigh slightly above the stifle.
Pulse Character	Strong and steady. Taken by relaxing the pressure of your finger against the pulsating artery.
Capillary Filling Time	Two seconds. Measured by pressing a finger against Bingo's gum tissue for a few seconds, then releasing the pressure suddenly and recording the time taken for the pink color to return to normal.

Normal Signs of a Healthy Spaniel (continued)

Skin Character	Normal skin can be detected by picking up a fold of skin over his shoulder, and without hurting him, stretching it upward about an inch (2.5 cm) or two, then releasing it. It should suddenly snap back into place and regain its normal contour.
Skin Appearance	Smooth and clean, with about the same hair cover all over.
Mouth	Open his mouth and observe the odor of his breath. It should smell like dog food and his gums and tongue should be about the same color as your own tongue. Look for tarter buildup on his teeth.
Ears	Pick up his ears and sniff his ear canals. Look inside each ear using a strong light, but don't poke cotton swabs into the canal.
Scooting	Pick up his tail and observe his anus.

The First Examination

Bingo's first examination should include a careful assessment of his heart and lungs using a stethoscope. His temperature should be taken and recorded, the color of his mucous membranes should be evaluated, his teeth and throat checked, and perhaps you might hear a remark about his bite. His ears should be checked with an otoscope and his feet examined for broken nails. He should be weighed and his weight recorded for future reference. Notes should be made relative to his general health.

After the examination is completed ask the doctor if Bingo's heart and lungs sound normal. Let the clinician know that you want to be included, that Bingo isn't a commodity but a living, breathing member of your family and you are interested in his health. Don't settle for a report given by a technician in an offhand manner or worse yet, a printout. Veterinarians are human professionals and their time is valuable, but so is Bingo's health. If the doctor doesn't have time for a brief discussion and a few questions from you, find another one who has time for you and Bingo.

An English Springer puppy calculating a long step.

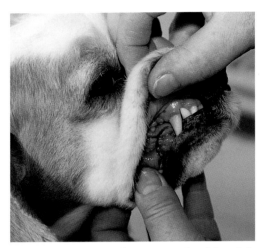

This Cocker Spaniel's gums are healthy pink and his teeth are shiny clean.

Only one type of good health exists but spaniels are subject to many illnesses. In order to help Bingo maintain his usual state of good health, we must know what constitutes wellness. That requires you to clearly evaluate his form and function. A logical place to begin is to list his normal vital signs because, since sickness is the absence of good health, any deviation from these standards may be a sign of illness.

What to Look For

To be a good owner, observe closely, record accurately, and respond to what you see by calling for help in a timely manner. Unless you are a graduate veterinarian you can't be expected to diagnose Bingo's illness, but you can recognize the differences between normal and abnormal. Bingo can't tell you verbally where he hurts but you may save him some

suffering and save money as well by performing an at-home examination and comparing what you see against the normal standards. Note the results of your observations to each item listed because a disorder can be signaled by more than one deviation from normal. When the clinician asks you on the phone how your spaniel is acting, you will have the answers to his questions and sometimes without seeing Bingo, the veterinarian will suggest whether or not he needs to come in for examination.

✔ Excessive water consumption may be a sign of diarrhea, vomiting, fever, or it may be the sign of several systemic diseases. Don't guess about his water consumption. Measure it and report the amount to your veterinarian.

✔ When he urinates and you observe his urine to be dark yellow or orange and perhaps thicker than you would expect, the problem might be associated with his diet, water consumption, or a dangerous kidney disease. If it contains blood, call immediately for an appointment with your veterinarian.

✔ If Bingo winces and resists having his mouth opened he will probably have halitosis as well. On examination you will probably find infected teeth, a tongue wound, gum tumors, or other deformities. It's time to call for professional help.

✔ Look over Bingo's skin for lumps and bumps of all sizes, hairless or reddened areas. Note their location and whether or not he is scratching at them. If his skin doesn't snap back into place after you've checked its character, that's a sign of dehydration and should tell you that further examinations are needed. He might have diarrhea that you haven't observed or maybe he's been vomiting and you haven't noticed it. Dehydration could be the

Grass awns frequently cause ear infections.

sign of a digestive disorder that you can treat at home or it might signal a serious disease that needs laboratory tests to diagnose. If his skin is red and inflamed with spots of hair missing and is accompanied by incessant licking or scratching, call your veterinarian for an appointment. The diagnosis may range from flea saliva allergy to demodectic mange. It might signal a systemic problem or topical disease but it does warrant your immediate attention.

✔ If his stool is liquid or softer than normal, look for mucus and blood in it. Diarrhea may be caused by a simple digestive upset or some bug or varmint that Bingo has found and eaten, but it might be cause for alarm.

✔ If he continually or intermittently scratches his ears or if they have a foul odor, and you see a soft wax buildup with your naked eye, he may have any of several serious problems such as otitis (bacterial ear canal infection). That condition may be associated with ear mites, lacerations in the ear canal, or foreign bodies such as grass awns lodged in the ear. Call for help.

✔ If he limps on one foot it might be caused by a small burr lodged in a hair mat between his toes or it might be caused by injury or it could be an early sign of a congenital deformity.

✔ If he's squinting and tearing excessively and you examine his eye carefully, you might discover the spines of a grass awn sticking out from under his third eyelid. Don't fool with such evidence because if the awn remains there for even a few hours, it may result in a corneal ulcer that will require extensive therapy to cure. Call for help.

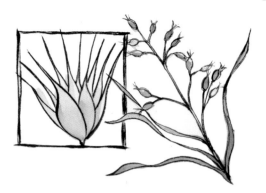

✔ If he coughs chronically and frequently, have him examined. It might be nothing more than an allergy or it might signal a heart problem.

✔ Discharge from his nose might alert you to a foreign body lodged in his nostril or a sinus infection, or nothing more than an allergy.

✔ Pale gums might mean he is anemic and should tell you that laboratory examinations are needed.

✔ A persistent fever of more than 2 degrees means that he needs further examination. It might be a sign of systemic disease or it might be the aftermath of a beesting. Call for advice.

✔ If he's scooting and you find fecal mats in his anal hair they can easily be treated by trimming the hair with clippers or scissors. If he's scooting and has no hair mats, his problem is likely impacted anal sacs. Ask your veterinarian to teach you how to express them at home because the problem will likely recur and the condition should respond to home therapy.

Internet Therapy

No matter how sure you are of the nature of his illness, don't guess about his health. Don't ever medicate Bingo with leftover medicine

A Cocker waiting for the rest of the team.

from a previous illness or human medicine that you've bought over the counter at the drugstore. Above all, don't give him home remedies you've heard about or read about on the Internet. The Internet provides a world at our fingertips. We can learn about the signs of diseases and therapy for those diseases as well. It's always fun to read what people have to say and sometimes it's tempting to read and respond without thinking any further. However, until a computer is able to see and palpate a canine patient, the value of its information is limited. Diagnosticians must witness the patient's responses to palpation, feel the character of the pulse, and call upon past experience and the innumerable professional books and journals they have read, and results of laboratory examinations must be considered. I have no argument with articles published on the Internet or the authenticity of individual opinions but a conscientious spaniel owner must know the authors and their creditability before they can be taken seriously. Even then, they are nothing more than guidelines to follow.

Common Serious Infectious Diseases

The following diseases can be controlled in healthy dogs by vaccination. All dogs need not be vaccinated in the same way because no single vaccination schedule fits all spaniels. Some veterinarians today are antibody testing all dogs before vaccinating. Ask your veterinarian his or her opinion about using multivalent vaccines at preselected intervals as opposed to testing and vaccinating for specific diseases. Above all, don't just follow advice that you found on the Internet. One generality does hold true, however: If a vaccine is given at weaning time or before, a booster should be given at a later date. Please consult your veterinarian before any home vaccination program is adopted.

Canine Distemper (CD)

Distemper is not often seen today because of the quality of modern vaccines. It is caused by a virulent virus and is spread by contact or airborne respiratory particles such as those that emanate from sneezing. Among the signs are coughing, loss of appetite, high fever, foul nasal discharge, and later, convulsions and death.

Canine Hepatitis (ICH or CAV-1)

Hepatitis is another viral disease, sometimes without visible signs. It is primarily liver disease but other vital organs are included as well. It is spread about the same as CD, and often results in death. Signs include fever, lethargy, sometimes vomiting and cloudy corneas commonly known as blue eye.

Leptospirosis (Lepto)

Lepto is primarily a disease of the kidneys and is spread from animal to animal by infected urine. Signs are usually walking with back arched, dark yellow or bloody-appearing urine, loss of appetite, and high fever.

Kennel Cough or Tracheobronchitis

Kennel Cough is caused by several bacteria, one of which is *Bordetella bronchiseptica*. Viruses, which also are found in some cases, include parainfluenza, distemper, CAV-2, and others. Antibiotics may help but no sure cure is available.

Parvovirus (Parvo)

Parvo is another virulent viral disease. It is transmitted through the feces of an infected dog and is often fatal in young puppies. Successful supportive therapy must be aggressive and continuous until a response is seen. Some dogs survive only to suffer heart disease and/or failure. Stools of infected dogs may contain virile Parvo agents for many months and common disinfectants are rarely effective.

Coronavirus

Coronavirus appears similarly to Parvo and can be specifically diagnosed by blood tests. Treatment regimes are similar as well and the fatality rate is about the same as with Parvo.

Lyme Disease

This disorder is cause by the bacterium *Borrelia burgodorferi*. It is named after Lyme County, Connecticut, where it was first

An English Springer Spaniel bursting with good health.

reported, but the disease has spread to virtually all the 50 states. It is transmitted by blood-sucking parasites; the signs are fever, sluggishness, joint swelling, and pain. It is diagnosed with difficulty but a blood test will help and a vaccine is available.

Rabies

This horrible, fatal disease is often thought to be totally under control but it still exists in the 48 contiguous states of America as well as Canada and Mexico. Surges of rabies outbreaks are discovered in wild carnivores that act as reservoirs for the virus. The virus is fatal to every infected individual, both two- and four-legged varieties. Vaccination of dogs for this disease is mandated by ordinances in most states, counties, and cities in the United States.

Ectoparasites include the flea, louse, tick, and mite.

External Parasites

External parasites include fungi, fleas, ticks, mites, and lice. They live on and within the skins of dogs and cause general itching and scratching. Always think of parasites first when Bingo scratches excessively.

Fleas

These pests are the most common external parasite of dogs. The adult flea lacerates the dog's skin and laps up the serum that oozes forth. Fleas are diagnosed by use of a flea comb, which has teeth set quite close together and when passed though the dog's coat, it traps the fleas and they can be seen with the naked eye. Adult fleas are easy to kill but the problems that arise from infestation are not as easily handled. They act as secondary hosts to tapeworms and thus, a second parasite may be introduced to Bingo. Flea saliva is highly allergenic and often causes a serious inflammatory process.

Life cycle: Fleas' life cycle is a problem. Adults feast on Bingo's blood, then they hop off and lay their eggs on the lawn or in your carpet. The larva hatch, pupate into adults, and each adult finds Bingo or another animal on which to catch a brief ride.

Therapy: Therapy includes many new products. Some are given to your spaniel orally;

others are applied to his skin. The chemical is absorbed and kills the adult fleas when they drink the animal's blood. Ask your veterinarian what type of control you should use on Bingo but don't buy and use over-the-counter products without professional advice and remember that use of more than one product can be toxic.

Ticks

These parasites bury their tiny heads into the skin of their hosts and suck blood for several days. Engorged female ticks then release, fall to the ground or carpet, lay thousands of eggs, each of which hatches to begin the life cycle again. Some ticks, such as brown dog ticks, use the dog for each stage of their lives, but most species use another mammal as secondary host for the immature stages of their lives.

Treatment: Treatment consists of removing the adult tick by means of tweezers and gentle, continuous pulling. Always wear a latex glove when removing a tick because tick-borne diseases can affect humans. Drop the tick into a container of alcohol to kill it and be careful not to squash it in the process. If the tick's head remains in Bingo's skin, don't panic—simply clip the hair and clean the area with alcohol daily for a few days. Some new products are highly

A Sussex waiting for further instructions.

effective in tick control as well as flea control. Ask your veterinarian for advice.

Fungi

These pesky plants grow on the surface of dog's skin and some can be transmitted to humans, which makes them more important. They cause itchy, red, hairless skin lesions that sometimes take a circular form. (That's why they are called *ringworm*.) They can be diagnosed by skin scraping that is observed with a microscope and sometimes they are cultured to identify. Treatment is by topical or oral fungicides. Cure doesn't mean control because many dogs are reinfected time and again.

Mange

This itchy skin disease is caused by several different types of microscopic mites known as *Demodex*, *Psoroptes*, and *Sarcoptes*. Those microscopic mites burrow in the outer layers of skin and cause intense inflammation, loss of hair, serum oozing, and secondary bacterial infection. Treatment may involve nutritional improvement, topical and/or systemic drugs to kill the mites and possibly anti-inflammatory drugs to control the itching.

Ear Mites

Those little brutes known as *Otodectes* may cause Bingo no end of misery. They are large enough to be seen with a magnifying glass and they live deep in the ear canals where they reproduce and cause intense itching, head shaking, and self destruction. Treatment includes thorough ear cleaning, agents to kill the mites, and sometimes anti-inflammatory drugs.

Lice

Lice live on the exterior of the spaniel's skin and coat. They are tiny bloodsucking pests that cause intense itching and scratching and are usually treated with medicated baths and special insecticides (powders or liquids). Lice lay their eggs (nits) on the shafts of hair, where they are easily found.

Internal Parasites

Roundworms (Ascarid)

Roundworm adults live in a dog's small intestine and lay eggs that are passed in Bingo's stool. A few days later, those eggs are infective to other dogs that sniff the infested stool; humans can be infested under certain circumstances. *Ascarid* larvae migrate through the spaniel's body before they mature and they may migrate into unborn puppies if a pregnant female dog is infested. The adult roundworm is easily killed with various drugs but overuse or improper dosage of these drugs is extremely dangerous.

Tapeworm life-cycle, including adult, egg-filled segments, and the flea.

Hookworms (Ancyclostoma)

Hookworms thrive in warm climates and can infest children under special circumstances. Hookworm adults live in the intestine of the dog and lay eggs that pass in the stool. The eggs hatch into larva that penetrate a dog's skin, migrate in the tissues and eventually into the gut, and mature into adults. The adults suck blood from their host and in heavy infestations this parasite can cause death of young puppies. Oral medication will kill the adult parasites but reinfestation is possible.

Tapeworms

These pests are two-host parasites; they aren't transmitted directly from dog to dog but require a secondary host to complete their life cycle. The secondary hosts can be fleas, birds, or many mammals. When the dog eats the secondary host's tissues, it becomes infested. The tapeworm head or scolex attaches to the lining of the dog's gut and the tapeworm's body can grow to many feet/meters long. The adult tapeworm's body is made up of hundreds of tiny segments, each of which contains scores of eggs. A segment breaks off, passes in the stool, is picked up by a secondary host, and the life-cycle is continued.

Check Bingo's anal area occasionally for tiny white segments. They are about the size and shape of grains of rice. Oral medication is used to successfully treat this pesky parasite but beware of over-the-counter medications; some of them are quite dangerous in the hands of a novice.

Heartworms

Heartworms are the bane of field dogs, especially shorthaired ones. Spaniels are just

This Welsh Springer dam and her puppies are relaxing between play times.

as susceptible to infestation but their coat sometimes protects them from mosquitoes, and the mosquito is the secondary host for heartworm larvae. Heartworm adults can grow to a length of a foot (30 cm) and dozens of heartworms living in Bingo's heart and major arteries can cause his death. Heartworms are prevented by monthly administration of oral medication after Bingo has been tested by the veterinarian and has been found free of preexisting infestation.

Coccidiosis

This intestinal disease of young dogs is caused by microscopic protozoa such as *isospora*. Its signs are persistent diarrhea and it is diagnosed by finding the oocysts (eggs) in the stool.

Parasite Therapy

Treating all puppies alike, whether or not they are infested, is almost as bad as not treating them at all. If Bingo was raised by a professional breeder, it is unlikely that he had any of the parasites discussed above. Good breeders know all about parasites and have too much invested in their breeding stock to take unnecessary risks. The best advice is to buy your spaniel from a reputable breeder, depend on your veterinarian for guidance, and don't guess about what drugs to use or when to use them. Your veterinarian will ask for a stool sample when Bingo is a puppy. The sample will be checked for worm eggs and advice will be given accordingly. Some newer drugs may prevent heartworms and a plethora of other parasites. Don't try to learn all the ways to *treat* parasites but trust your veterinarian's advice for *prevention*.

Nonpreventable Diseases

Some diseases of spaniels aren't preventable by vaccination or other means but those conditions may be treatable if and when they occur.

Common Diseases

Disease	Incidence and Age	Cause	Signs
Atopy	All spaniels, young adults	Allergy to pollens or specific foods	Intense itching that's not associated with parasites
Cataracts	Cockers, young adults	Hereditary	Gradual loss of vision, clouding of lens of eyes
Diabetes mellitus	All spaniels, middle age	Insulin deficiency; hereditary predisposition	Obesity, lethargy, thirst, increased appetite
Distichiasis	English Springer, Cockers, any age	Hereditary	Abnormal presence of secondary row of eyelashes
Double teeth	All spaniels, seen soon after teething is complete	Hereditary; often due to downsizing of some breeds	Baby teeth fail to drop out as adult teeth are acquired
Ectropion	All spaniels, young to middle age	Hereditary; excessive skin in orbital region	Eyelids roll outward, weepy eyes, chronic conjunctivitis
Epilepsy	Field Spaniel, Cocker, Springer, youths to middle age	Hereditary	Gradual, progressive, convulsive disorder
Glaucoma	Cocker, Springer, youths	Hereditary	Pain due to increased intraocular pressure
Hip Dysplasia	All spaniels, middle age to later	Hereditary, abnormal hip joint formation	Hind leg lameness, difficulty in getting up, pain when handled
Hypothyroidism	Field Spaniel and others, middle age	Hereditary	Lethargy, obesity, skin problems
Otitis Externa	All spaniels, all ages	Bacterial infections due to lack of air circulation in pendulant, heavily haired ears	Foul odor, wet ear canals, excess wax and pus exuding, chronic scratching; sometimes accompanied by ear hematoma
Progressive Retinal Atrophy	English Springer and others, young adults	Hereditary loss of function of retina of eyes	Gradual loss of vision resulting in blindness
Undershot jaw or malocclusion	Clumber, Cocker, and Irish Water Spaniel, all ages	Hereditary abnormal mandibular growth	Lower teeth spaced well forward from uppers

First Aid for Spaniels

Hopefully you will never be faced with an emergency involving your beloved pet but in case you are, you should be prepared. Don't fail to muzzle Bingo before you attempt to help him because any dog, no matter how docile and loving, can be expected to react to pain by biting the person handling him. In case you don't have your first aid kit with you, tie his muzzle closed with his leash, a shoestring, belt, necktie, or strip of cloth.

Shock

Shock is a serious and potentially fatal condition and should be diagnosed and treated by a professional if at all possible. In case Bingo has been hit by a car, cover him with blankets or coats, soothe him with quiet words, pet him, and reassure him. Take out your emergency card and, using your cell phone, call the nearest animal emergency clinic or your veterinarian and ask for instructions. Don't try to straighten an injured and displaced leg, and don't try to pick him up until directed to do so.

Artificial Respiration and Cardiopulmonary Resuscitation

AR (artificial respiration) should be administered only if the patient is unconscious.

✔ Lay Bingo on his right side, open his mouth, and, with a pocket handkerchief wipe out any mucus or blood.

✔ Close his mouth, place your lips tightly over his muzzle, and blow into his nostrils until you can see his chest raise slightly. Remove your mouth and let him exhale. Repeat this procedure about 10 times per minute.

═══ CHECKLIST ═══

First Aid Kit for Spaniels

1. Card with emergency numbers to call
2. Piece of ¼-inch (6-mm) nylon cord about 4 feet (1.2 m) long to use for muzzle or tourniquet
3. Roll of 3-inch (7.6-cm) bandage
4. Roll of 2-inch (5.1-cm) adhesive tape
5. Tube of antibiotic cream
6. Eyewash or artificial tears
7. Small bottle of 2 percent hydrogen peroxide
8. Blunt-tipped scissors
9. Styptic stick for torn toenails
10. Rectal thermometer
11. Tweezers or cheap pair of hemostats
12. Bingo's normal vital signs chart

Proper placement of a strap or rope muzzle.

Tourniquets

Do not use a tourniquet unless the hemorrhage from the wound can't be stopped with pressure.

✔ If a tourniquet is used, use a shoestring, belt, necktie, or strip of cloth.

✔ Place the tourniquet between the wound and the patient's heart and tie it to itself.

✔ Then place a stick or similar object in the loop of the tourniquet and twist it.

✔ Hold it in place and loosen it for a few seconds every 15 minutes.

The Clumber Spaniel is willing and able to retrieve all day at a reasonable pace.

✔ If he is small, be careful that you don't overinflate his lungs.

✔ Check his heartbeat by placing a hand tightly over the left side of his chest. If a heartbeat is felt, continue artificial respiration.

CPR: If no heartbeat is detected, have a friend help you and begin CPR (cardiopulmonary resuscitation). Draw his foreleg forward and in the position where his elbow was, push downward on his chest to compress it to about half its normal thickness. Then release the pressure suddenly. Repeat the compression about every second until the heartbeat returns.

Minor Lacerations

The hair surrounding small wounds, abrasions, and scratches that don't require veterinary treatment should be clipped closely to help prevent bacterial contamination. The wound should be cleaned with soap and water and left to air-dry and heal. If the wound is located where Bingo's tongue can't reach it, apply first aid cream.

Puncture Wounds

Punctures often occur in a hard-running spaniel and you should be prepared when Bingo accidentally runs into a sharp stick, nail, or bent wire. Calm him with soft talk and carefully examine the puncture. If a penetrating object remains in his flesh, don't remove it—plucking a sliver of wood from a deep wound may produce a hemorrhage and be counterproductive for another reason as well: a sharp stick may leave splinters in the wound without your knowledge. Have a friend drive you to your veterinarian or the closest emergency veterinary clinic and have the situation evaluated professionally and the object removed.

A pair of Cocker puppies looking for mischief.

Extensive Wounds

Wide or deep wounds should also be seen by a veterinarian without any first aid treatment except to prevent your spaniel from getting his tongue into the act. In case the wound is accompanied by excessive bleeding, find the source of the hemorrhage and apply finger pressure to the blood vessel. If the wound is in an area that can be bandaged, place a pressure bandage over the wound, hair and all, and get Bingo to the veterinarian without delay.

Heatstroke

This potential killer occurs mostly in the summer when the outside temperatures are over 90°F (32°C) but it may be seen anytime when a heavily coated spaniel (or any dog) is left in a closed car that's sitting in the sun. The inside car temperature can quickly reach well over 100°F (37.8°C). Heatstroke is manifested by rapid, open-mouth panting, production of thick, stringy saliva, bright red mucous membranes, and sometimes coma. Cool Bingo quickly by getting him outside into the shade and soak his coat with cold water. If possible, place him in a tub and cover him with water but if he is unconscious, be sure to elevate and hold his head. Take his temperature and call your veterinarian for further instructions.

Poisoning

Poisoning should be treated by a professional. Call your veterinarian to alert the staff that you're on your way, then hasten to the clinic. If the product consumed is known, take the container with you. If you can't reach a veterinarian, follow the label directions on the product.

Convulsions

Convulsions may follow poisoning or they may be caused by epilepsy, a hereditary disorder that's rather common in spaniels. To protect Bingo from harming himself, steady him, wrap his body in a large towel or blanket, don't move him until he's acting normally, and don't try to pull his tongue out. If the convulsion is caused by epilepsy he will recover within a few minutes. Take him to your veterinarian for diagnosis and treatment to prevent or minimize future attacks.

Squinting

If Bingo squints his eye it may be a sign of some foreign material under the eyelid. Tilt his head back and hold his muzzle shut with one hand while you roll the upper eyelid back with your finger of your other hand. If nothing is seen, flush the eye several times with artificial tears. Have him examined at the earliest possible time.

Reasons for Surgically Neutering (Castrating) Males

✔ Neutering does not halt development of the male's mental or physical development.
✔ Neutering males doesn't cause obesity! Only an excess of dietary calories and a lack of exercise will cause obesity in an otherwise healthy male dog.
✔ His personality will not change appreciably but he may mellow a bit because he now has one less distraction on his mind.
✔ He will usually stay home because the occasional scent of a bitch in season won't attract him to run away.
✔ Intact males are usually more aggressive than those that have been neutered.
✔ Neutered males are said to be more affectionate toward humans.
✔ Neutered males are said to be more predictable in multiple competitive events such as flyball or agility trials.
✔ A neutered male will not develop prostate cancer or testicular cancer.

Lameness

Most spontaneous limping is caused by pad injuries. Pick up Bingo's foot and examine his pads closely for lacerations or foreign bodies. If a thorn is found, pluck it out and squirt on some hydrogen peroxide. If the problem is a pad laceration, bandage the foot snuggly, extending the bandage up the leg a few inches/centimeters. Use plenty of tape and gauze or he'll have it off in a heartbeat. If the lameness is due to a torn toenail, apply a styptic stick firmly to the bleeding nail and hold it until the bleeding stops, then bandage the foot.

Stretchers

A stretcher can be fashioned out of a blanket, coat, or a big cardboard box. Don't ever handle an injured dog more than necessary. If carrying is necessary and no stretcher material is available, pick him up with one arm in front of his shoulders and the other behind his rump, and pull him snuggly to your chest.

Important: Be prepared for emergencies each time you leave home with Bingo. You never know what problems you might encounter in the countryside. Put together a small first aid kit in a nylon belt pouch and carry it alongside your cellular phone.

Spaying

Reasons Not to Spay

If your female spaniel is to be shown, she can't be spayed because AKC conformation shows are basically proving grounds for breeding quality. Some AKC competitions allow neutered males and spayed females to compete; others don't. To be sure that you fully understand the regulations that govern neutered males and spayed females, contact the AKC directly on the Internet or by mail.

Castration of Males

Male spaniel pets should be neutered at an early age with the same exceptions that were outlined for females. For conformation classes and certain other events, males must be intact.

Reasons for Spaying Before the First Heat

✔ The risk of surgery is minimized if spaying is done before the first heat.

✔ The cost of spaying a young bitch is less than the cost of spaying an older bitch, especially after she's come into heat a few times, and much less than one that has had puppies.

✔ A spayed bitch will never suffer from a very dangerous condition of older bitches known as pyometra (uterine infection).

✔ A bitch that is spayed before her first heat is virtually assured of being free from mammary cancer throughout her life.

✔ A spayed female will never experience estrus (heat) and therefore won't attract males for three weeks out of every six months.

✔ Contemporary research indicates that very early spaying (after about three months of age) does not interfere with maturing, training, working, or hunting.

✔ Spaying does not halt mental or physical development and all spayed females don't get fat. Obesity is caused by under-exercising and overeating in a healthy animal.

✔ Some dogs' temperaments are moderated by spaying.

However, if the spaniel is a companion pet and has no greater ambition than sharing your life, he can be neutered and will prove to be a better, more predictable pet, if he is neutered at an early age before certain bad habits develop.

Euthanasia

When it's necessary to accept the finality of death, euthanasia is not an easy way out. It is a humane way to end a life of pain and misery after you've done all things possible to extend Bingo's quality of life. You've taken the best advice throughout his life, provided good nutrition and medical care, and have always treated him as you would want to be treated. You have nothing for which to apologize.

When you see the truth of Bingo's pitiful condition in his cloudy eyes, it will be obvious to you that he is miserable. After you have read about giving comfort to your old spaniel and those suggestions have been used up and are no longer working, it's time to remember that this fine old spaniel trusted you to take charge of his life. The decision to give him up is yours, not his. A good friend deserves the best you can give and sometimes that is exactly what you don't want to supply.

Instead of taking him to the hospital, make an evening or early-morning appointment with your veterinarian to come to your house to perform this task. Spend a few minutes alone with Bingo to reassure him with soft words and quiet petting, then stay with him while the veterinarian places a tourniquet on his foreleg, slips a needle into the vein, and injects the lethal dose quickly and painlessly.

Plant a tree in his memory. Join a grief support group. Read the information related to loss of a cherished pet that's available on the Internet. Don't blame yourself for your final action but accept the responsibility for providing a final act of kindness and love for your old friend.

Old dogs have no pensions, no social security, and no Medicare card. They can't go to live with their children in Kansas or retire to an extended care facility. They don't have eyeglasses or hearing aids, canes, or walkers. They have only *you*! You took responsibility for your spaniel many years ago and have watched and marveled at Cindy's ability to cope with the problems of aging.

Aging Signs

She's gray around the muzzle and her eyesight is becoming dimmer. Her joints creak when she gets up and her coat is dry and mats easily. A chair she discovers in a new place confuses her and she forgets where her water dish is. Sometimes she leaks urine when she sleeps but is terribly embarrassed when she discovers what she has done. She lies in strange places and assumes strange positions. Her magnificent hearing is nearly gone. You want to do something for her to ease her struggle. What can you do?

✔ Have patience with her. Give her the consideration *you* would desire under similar circumstances.

✔ Continue to take her for walks but not too far. Watch to see if she wants to take time out along the way. Touch her gently when you want to get her attention.

✔ Her deafness is probably not total, so speak up.

✔ She suffers from nuclear sclerosis, a vision condition similar to cataracts, so don't take her to strange places in subdued light.

✔ Build ramps at the edge of stairs that she must climb.

✔ Cover tile floors with runners because she has a difficult time walking on slick surfaces.

✔ Provide her with several washable, thick mats to lie on. Bathroom rugs work very well. Put them in her favorite resting places; wash and replace them regularly.

✔ Never scold her when she leaves a damp spot behind.

✔ When you see her struggling to rise, lift her hind end gently to make getting started easier for her.

✔ Keep her nails trimmed and watch out for dewclaws that have overgrown into pads.

✔ Don't move household furniture because she has memorized all the landmarks and changes may cause her to bump into things.

✔ Stomp your feet when you near her place of rest so she will be able to feel vibrations and know that you're approaching.

A stair ramp is easy to build.

TO YOUR AGING SPANIEL

✔ Watch for signs of cognitive dysfunction and be aware that a geriatric dog may begin to bark for no reason, pace, and urinate and defecate in inappropriate places.

✔ Have her health evaluated semiannually by your veterinarian and follow his suggestions related to specific tests for geriatric diseases that require special therapy.

✔ Be especially watchful for dental problems and gum tumors; often a foul odor will lead you to a mouth problem.

A few old bath mats will add to your old Spaniel's comfort.

✔ Be aware of sebaceous skin cysts and other small tumors. Ask your veterinarian about them.

✔ Clean the mucus accumulation from her eyes daily with a damp cotton ball. Place a drop of artificial tears in her eyes a couple of times daily.

✔ Check her elbow calluses regularly for serum seepage and infection.

✔ Watch the nature of her urine and feces to be sure neither is abnormal and report any abnormalities seen to your veterinarian.

✔ Give her fresh, cool drinking water several times daily.

✔ Ask your veterinarian about supplements and a special geriatric diet. Feed small meals several times a day. Warm her food slightly to make it more palatable. If her appetite wanes, mix a small amount of bouillon in her food before you warm it.

✔ Ask your veterinarian about medication that will relieve her arthritic pain.

✔ Clip and wash her flews (jaw skin folds) regularly to prevent infection in the folds of loose skin.

✔ Clip her facial and ear hair regularly to prevent persistent dampness related to drooling and drinking.

✔ Clip the hair from around her anus to prevent feces from sticking in mats that accumulate there.

✔ Clip her body all over in warm weather to prevent matting and fly strikes from occurring.

✔ Advise visitors to supervise their children because her tolerance has worn thin and she may have less patience than previously with kids.

Books

American Kennel Club. *The Complete Dog Book, 19th Edition.*
New York: Howell Book House, 2004.
(Contains all 146 breeds with breed standards, canine sports, trials, and showing information.)

Coile, Caroline. *Encyclopedia of Dog Breeds, 2nd Edition.* Hauppauge, NY: Barron's Educational Series, Inc., 2005.

Yamazaki, Tetsu. *Legacy of the Dog.* San Francisco: Chronicle Books, 1995.

Periodicals

Dog World Magazine
P.O. Box 37186
Boone, IA 50037-0186
1-800-361-8056

A Clumber waiting for his master.

AKC Gazette
51 Madison Avenue
New York, NY 10010

Dog Fancy
P.O. Box 53264
Boulder, CO 80322-3264

Organizations

American Kennel Club
260 Madison Avenue
New York, NY 10016
www.akc.org

American Veterinary Medicine Association
1931 N Meacham Road, Suite 100
Schaumburg, IL 60173
avmainfo@avma.org

American Water Spaniel National Club
1040-74½ Avenue North
Brooklyn Park, MN 55444
www.americanwaterspanielclub.org

Clumber Spaniel Club of America, Inc.
6585 Rosemoor Street
Pittsburgh, PA 15217-2742
secretary@clumbers.org

Cocker Spaniel Club, Inc.
30 Cardinal Loop
Crossville, TN 38555-5899
ascsecy@charter.net

English Cocker Spaniel Club of America, Inc.
P.O. Box 252
Hales Corners, WI 53130-0252
www.ecsca.org

English Springer Spaniel Field Trial Association, Inc.
E 9538 Kanaman Road
New London, WI 54961
mparszew@athenet.net

Field Spaniel Society of America
W845 Highway 20
East Troy, WI 53120-0901
terryfssa@yahoo.com

Irish Water Spaniel Club of America
1930 Marion Avenue
Novato, CA 94945-1755
clubs.akc.org/iwsc

A momma English Cocker with her youngsters.

Sussex Spaniel Club of America
2160 Willow Lane
Lexington, OH 44904-9718
www.sussexspaniels.org

Welsh Springer Spaniel Club of America, Inc.
783 Ellington Farm Road
Manson, NC 27553
daytimews@aol.com

About the Authors

Hans and Evamaria Ullmann are well-known animal photographers and spaniel experts. Dan Rice is a veterinarian who has written a number of books on dogs for Barron's.

Cover Photos

Norvia Behling: inside front cover and Isabelle Francais: front cover, back cover, and inside back cover.

Photo Credits

Norvia Behling: 7, 10, 21, 34, 35 (top), 39, and 56; Kent Dannen: 4, 6, 12, 13, 15, 17, 22 (top), 23, 24, 26, 27, 28, 29, 31, 38, 40, 42, 43, 45 (top), 48, 54, 62, 64, 66, 67, 71, 75, 76, 81, and 86; Tara Darling: 2–3, 5, 19, 25, 33, 35 (bottom), 36, 49, 57, 58 (top), 59, 61, 68, 69, 78, and 79; Isabelle Francais: 9, 11, 16, 18, 20, 30, 32, 37, 41, 46, 47, 52, 53, 55, 58 (bottom), 60, 65, 72, 73, 83, 87, 92, and 93; Pets by Paulette: 8 and 22 (bottom); and Connie Summers: 45 (bottom).

Important Note

This pet owner's manual tells the reader how to buy or adopt, and care for spaniels. The author and publisher consider it important to point out that the advice given in this book is meant primarily for normally developed dogs of excellent physical health and good character.

Anyone who adopts a fully grown dog should be aware that the animal has already formed its basic impressions of human beings. The new owner should watch the animal carefully, including its behavior toward humans, and should meet the previous owner.

Caution is further advised in the association of children with dogs, in meeting with other dogs, and in exercising the dog without proper safeguards.

Even well-behaved and carefully supervised dogs sometimes do damage to someone else's property or cause accidents. It is therefore in the owner's interest to be adequately insured against such eventualities, and we strongly urge all dog owners to purchase a liability policy that covers their dog(s).

Second English-language edition published in 2006 by Barron's Educational Series, Inc. First English-language edition published in 1982 by Barron's Educational Series, Inc.

All inquiries should be addressed to:
Barron's Educational Series, Inc.
250 Wireless Boulevard
Hauppauge, NY 11788
www.barronseduc.com

Library of Congress Catalog Card No. 2005050707

ISBN-13: 978-0-7641-3139-4
ISBN-10: 0-7641-3139-7

Library of Congress Cataloging-in-Publication Data
Ullmann, Hans-Jochen.
   [Spaniels. English]
   Spaniels : everything about history, purchase, care, nutrition, training, and behavior / Hans J. Ullmann, Evamaria Ullmann, Dan Rice.—2nd English-language ed.
      p. cm.—(A Complete pet owner's manual)
   Includes bibliographical references (p.) and index.
   ISBN 0-7641-3139-7
   1. Spaniels. I. Ullmann, Evamaria. II. Rice, Dan, 1933– III. Title. IV. Series.

SF429.S7U4413   2006
639.752'4—dc22   2005050707

Printed in China
9 8 7 6 5 4 3 2 1